OH, T\
the HORRI
ASYMMETRIC WARFARE
in the world

A SYNOPSIS OF EVENTS
from 2020 - 2024 THAT MAY
PROVE TO BE THE MOST
DEVASTATINGLY CONSEQUENTIAL
and most Destructive of Democracy
in the HISTORY of the WORLD
Including anecdotes from
SIGNIFICANT EARLIER WRITERS
and
THOUGHTS FROM PREVIOUS
TIMES

BY
Dr. MOSWEE M. PEACH

DIRECTOR BOOK PRESS

Printed in the United States of America

Published by: Director Book Press
USA

Library of Congress Cataloging - in - Publication Data
Attorneys, Resident, Moscow, Pyongyang, Mesmerize
HOW to *FAKE* AMERICA GREAT, AGAIN

A book by: DIRECTOR BOOK PRESS
ISBN 979 - 8 - 37063 - 743-8

First printing December 2022
Second Edition April 2023
3rd Edition September 2023
4th Edition December 5th, 2023
5th Edition and Printing September, 2024

TABLE OF CONTENTS

This book is an absolute must read to discover what has happened to our world in the past almost totally disastrous three plus years and has only gotten worse, not better, since Biden's election. I've read books written ten years ago when the GOP occupied the White House. Those seemed to be just as bad. But it is worse - much worse - even during the bad GOP years 10 years ago. The people in charge then, actually believed in the Rule of Law, the Constitution, institutions and the traditions that make up the Democratic government of the United States. There was a kind of unspoken TRUST in it all!

What we have run into here, apparently, is a group of people that no longer value the Constitution and may have no interest in it and may feel that the United States of America must reject all Rule of Law. They seem to feel the only thing that matters is the grasp of absolute power and control. They think that three equal branches with powers of checks and balances to regulate the other two branches is meaningless. Just because the Constitution, laws and regulations may say that they must do certain things - somewhere they seem to have it in their heads that's all actually irrelevant - If they just decide that they don't want to do it. The bottom line is: who the hell is going to stop them from not doing it? Well, you will see as you go through this book what a dilemma this has turned out to be. And, by far, it is not over! In just one year the world is in a total disaster and getting devastatingly worse by the day.

A goal of this book might be to bring a generally broader awareness to light of what has seemingly been going on to a larger spectrum of the population so that perhaps, from that, appropriate actions may be taken that might eventually turn this situation around and get us aimed at a much better place. We need EVERYTHING to rid us of these many bad CANCERS.

WHAT is Meant by ASYMMETRIC WARFARE?

When two forces are pushing an object in opposition to each other, if they are pretty much balanced, it can be assumed that the motion of the object will be much of a back and forth near the starting position. However, if you start the "contest" with one powered by a small spring and the other powered by a 400 horsepower gasoline engine, well, you can see how that would turn out without any need to actually perform the experiment.

Think of a game of football. You have two teams that are pretty well matched both offensively and defensively. They both have very talented quarterbacks and pass receivers. They have pretty well-balanced lines - both offensive and defensive. They both have very effective back fields - again both offensively and defensively. So, as the game is played for four quarters, there is a give and take, a back and forth, a score that may go up for one team and then later for the other. The outcome at the end may result in very similar scores. Which team wins, then, may only be a matter of the time played or which team played offense last or other incidental events along the way.

However, even under these conditions, if you have judges and linesmen that have been "paid off" to call penalties on one team and not the other, I almost guarantee you that the outcome will be very lopsided with one team having a very large score and the other team having a very small score. The outcome will, in no way, reflect the well-established abilities of either of those two teams. So, you might say that this kind of game and outcome was the result of an asymmetric war. The asymmetry of the judging tipped the game way off balance to become a rout instead of an exciting game of skill and balance! Who would actually be excited to see such a "Rout"?

2   We just finished the 2022 winter Olympics in Beijing China (a very odd place to have such a peaceful sporting event, based upon China's asymmetric place in world history at this very moment). There were events like one-person Bobsled and Luge where the gold medal was determined by 2 tenths of a second out of a total of about 48 seconds for the race. That is about 0.4 percent of the total time for the run. Not much asymmetry there! That 0.4% is based upon very small differences in the run, such as tapping the wall with the sled for a brief fraction of a second on a curve or down a straight line during the run.

Not just as a nation, but more likely as people, we love to watch very closely matched sporting events and competitions because of the excitement that exists when two closely matched teams vie back and forth to gain the lead even for brief periods of time. No one likes to watch a rout! Boring! There is absolutely no excitement and certainly no reason to even bother sticking it out to the end. People, basically, as part of humanity, abhor asymmetric outcomes - perhaps it is as simple as just being totally unfair. Not according to Hoyle.

Apparently, human nature abhors a ROUT, a bully, or a total AH! What is it about "fairness" and a sense of fair play that so inspires us? Do unto others as we would have others do unto us? Bottom line, let's face it, nobody likes cheats, charlatans, thieves, or con men! No one cares to see other people getting something for nothing. No one wants to feel they have been cheated, robbed, slighted or "taken advantage of".

Are these innate human values, or are they acquired by upbringing, education, training, socialization, "getting along to get along" or what? There must be, from years of living together in large concentrations, such as in cities, a sense of normality that must have evolved over time from dire, disastrous previous situations that established that we all must behave within a certain range of norms to make sure that crowded civilizations are able to survive. Perhaps, this is an instinct for survival that evolved over time. Somewhere, most of us have developed a sense of humanity and empathy for the plight of others. Perhaps, also a conscience about something called "right and wrong". So, what if someone just decides that they are going to go against the norm and disobey everything that makes civilizations work? What do you have then, and what would it be called other than an abhorrent behavior?

Perhaps they would be a criminal, a thief, a bully, a psychopath, a deviant, a narcissist or even the devil himself. Clearly, they would be considered to be totally Immoral. The immoral person knows the difference between right and wrong, but has realized that by ignoring all of the rules that make civilizations work, he is able to take tremendous advantage of others by the use of this kind of asymmetric behavior. They fully intend to use this immoral behavior to take horrendous advantage over someone else, an entire nation or a group of nations. The irony is that these people very quickly become known as outcasts from society - they are totally derelict - a priori - criminals! Perhaps, even Pariahs!

Adolf Hitler was a famous example of this kind of behavior. I can think of at least two more abhorrent deviants at this very moment. Can you name them? The problem seems to be that there are a very large number of deviant followers that are criminally challenged to even be able to either recognize these persons as such or be able to discern that what they are doing or standing for is totally destructive to not only their own lives but to those of the entire world and to the humanity that normally is part of the lives that they would choose to live

CHAPTER 2
SIMPLE EXAMPLES of ASYMMETRIC WARFARE

These are particularly difficult chapters to write because so much is happening, almost by the minute. Where to start? Well, let's start with the Fascist Authoritarian Dictatorship (FAD) states that have already been established in the past 6 years. I'm talking about Texas, Florida and, perhaps to a lesser extent, Georgia. During the peak of the Covid-19 Pandemic, the Governor of Florida signed laws and passed executive orders designed to prevent the practice of sensible common health practices to curb or curtail the spread of the deadly virus in schools as well as in the state at large. Banning mask mandates in schools, in crowded public places, crowded resorts, on cruise ships and other commonly used tourist locations is truly insane. Of course it's insane, so why did he do it and how does he get by with it? Ah, more on that in the following chapters - but, let's just say for now: because he can! It serves his purpose to establish that HE is the Boss!

The Governor of Florida signed a bill that "restricted" the use of the word "Gay". Why did he do that? To make it clear that he was the BOSS of the residents of the state and that they were not! Disney, one of the largest employers of the state, had stated that was not acceptable. He went after Disney, the company and the resort in Orlando. He made it clear that he would punish all of them as a lesson to every other company that disagreement would never be tolerated. They must learn who is the Dictator and who decides how they all must live!
This kind of "out of the ordinary" behavior is considered to be an asymmetrical kind of warfare because it goes against every "norm" that a democratic society has grown to expect!

Why do people go into public service? They generally go   5
to serve the public with a bit of shenanigans and profiteering
on the side. As despicable as that is, unfortunately, the public
has come to accept a small amount of that as a price to pay for
"getting the sausage made" for the betterment of the society.
But, when these politicians go to a style that not only doesn't
"get the sausage made" but instead makes your lives far more
miserable, if not even dangerous, you have crossed the line
into the realm of Asymmetric Warfare. That's a clear sign
you're in a FAD (Fascist Authoritarian Dictatorship) State!

Texas has passed the most heinous, despicable, death
causing anti-abortion law of all time and for all time. Instead of
Texas being the legal entity that would ban abortions, they
have made everyone in the state (or for that matter anywhere
else) into vigilantes. The law says that anyone may sue
anyone else for at least $10,000 for either having an abortion
or being a party to or aiding and abetting someone obtaining
an abortion. That could include taxi drivers, neighbors, Uber
or Lyft drivers, abortion clinic personnel and doctors, or even
informants who tell a person where they might find a back
alley practitioner. SCOTUS would not overrule this law even
though in normal courts of law - only people who are
personally aggrieved or directly harmed by some action have
standing in that court of law. Clearly, not one of these
vigilantes have standing because they are in no way harmed
by someone else's abortion! Clearly, this law must be struck
from the books as being totally unconstitutional. And yet, it
now appears that our SCOTUS has been completely corrupted,
and its entire function is totally controlled by the Fascist GOP
party as part of their complete takeover as a FAD State. This
can end everything that used to be decent or sane – forever!
These books have warned for decades to vote as if SCOTUS
depended upon it! Your entire lives depend upon it as well!

CHAPTER 3
How Does ASYMMETRIC WARFARE Work?

Where to start? There must be quite a number of studies on how dictators behave once they have gained their power. These must, in some way, deal with the effects that very deviant behavior has on normal thinking and living beings. Let's examine some very interesting aspects of this.

Society has apparently grown, over time, to establish some norms of behavior for everyone to follow, in order that the society will be able to continue to exist - essentially reasonably, peacefully - together. Of course, there tends to be some deviants to these norms, so society passes laws in order to deter, arrest, or completely stop these out of norm behaviors from occurring. Some laws, like transit laws, are necessary to reduce the risk of accidental deaths and injury from commonly used vehicles. The same applies to the use of guns, or any other potentially dangerous object or instrument of common use. Hopefully, these laws, if applied quickly and forcibly, will reduce the damage caused by deviants to society that intentionally break these laws and create destruction.

So, if you have rules for a society, in this case the Constitution, people who tend to get elected, are ones who want to make the society better, and go to congress to do that. It is clearly understood, by the norms and traditions, that you follow the rules and above all, act to defend the Constitution. But, what happens if someone has quite a different agenda - perhaps to totally destroy the Constitution, the norms and the traditions of a Government? How would they go about doing that? When put in that context, it's almost intuitive that the way to start is to not follow any of the norms, traditions or rules, and to show total disrespect for every norm of society.

The interesting part has to do with human nature. Even 7 when someone does something out of the norm, we assume they are acting normally. If somewhat more bizarre, we excuse the faux pas as a quirk of personality. In fact, we are so in tune with people always doing "the right thing" that we go to extreme lengths to believe that there is absolutely nothing unsavory that is being "pulled over" on us. Some of us tend to be more cynical and look for the worst possible reasons for bizarre behaviors. Much of this is based upon the history of some of the worst deviants in history. Hitler, Kim Jung-un and Putin come to mind very quickly. That is why a thorough education is so important to a well-oiled Democratic Society. We must thoroughly understand History lest we tend to repeat it. Bad history MUST NEVER BE REPEATED! A thoroughly classic education is required to keep that from happening.

Ok, where does this get us as a society? Recently, we have elected people who were "predictably" of the right frame of mind to have our best interests at heart. How did we know that? THEY TOLD US SO - OVER and OVER AGAIN! MAKE AMERICA GREAT AGAIN! As Patriots, we must save this nation from the Liberals and Communists. As Patriots, we MUST TAKE THIS NATION BACK! We must "FIGHT LIKE HELL" or we won't take our nation back. Back from what? Success? Being a history buff, I believe that I've heard these exact phrases from a period of time in Europe during the 1930's and early 1940's! They were NAZI slogans. When Germany went from a Democratic Republic to a Nazi Authoritarian Dictatorship (almost imperceptibly at first - step by step) Democracy slipped away leaving the inevitably dreaded Dictatorship. People, even then, thought, "Oh, this can't be right but what can I do about it?" My representative has to do something about it! Oh, by then, the representatives were in on "THE STEAL" So, step by step, it was all taken away!

8   Again, what does all this tell us about these and other "unusual situations?" When people have lived their entire lives living the good life in a Democracy, they have absolutely no idea how bad it can be living in a place like Putin's Russia or Kim Jong-un's North Korea. So, when seemingly deviant behavior happens, people tend to dismiss it "out of hand" as an aberration. We find ourselves in the following situations:

When DeSantis bans the wearing of face masks in schools or on tour ships - we are totally horrified. Why in the world would anyone - least of all, the Governor - require something so totally opposite to all common sense and sound health practices? BECAUSE HE CAN and HE KNOWS THAT HE CAN GET AWAY WITH IT! Cruelty is the thing! Pain is the Gain! The worse the pain, the better you know that he is the dictator and that you are not! The more you begin to get used to very unexpected and totally unreasonable things being imposed upon you the sooner he knows that YOU KNOW that he is absolutely in charge of your entire lives. You'll know how bad it's going to be! Again, CRUELTY IS THE CLEAR MESSAGE!

When DeSantis has an absurd law passed banning the use of the word 'GAY', Disney and Disney World take him on for a total absurdity and cruelty to not only Disney employees, their family and friends, but to every one of the 50 million visitors to their parks every year. Oh yes, Disney is one of the number one employers in Florida, a state with only 22.7 million residents. Normally, most people would say; "That is the very dumbest thing anyone could do to ruin the business income of the state." And, they would be right! CRUELTY IS THE GAME. You are now realizing the fact that this is the goal of a Fascist Dictator who tells you in no uncertain terms - you're the one to be RULED! This is the worst form of Asymmetric action!

We have now seen some examples of Asymmetric actions that are making huge differences in how people's perceptions

and behaviors are severely modified. This is an extremely
important example of how effective these tactics can be.

I could give you a thousand examples of Asymmetric action to either modify or totally control the minds and bodies of those RULED! But with asymmetric action, there is an even more sinister component! That is this crucial fact: The "other side" does not believe in doing those kinds of asymmetric things! Simply said, they tend to believe in the Rule of Law and in decent, Democratic behavior - playing fair and with integrity. So, not only are they grossly shocked that someone would even consider doing those vile things, they are also constrained from fighting "fire with fire" because their codes of honor will not permit them to stoop that low - even to survive!

This additional fact, alone, makes the use of Asymmetric action to be so GD effective as a means to control populations in the style of a dictator. The decent people want to preserve peace and dignity of life as being more important than even a good life itself. If the deviation is small, they don't believe that going low to survive is worth the price of GOING LOW to survive. Voila! That is why 'would be' dictators prefer to use asymmetric action to accomplish their ends. By those means, they are able to achieve their goals within the bounds of the Democratic Laws and Norms of their Government.

For example, when you use illegal faux militias with guns to intimidate the population on the streets, it is difficult for ordinary people (whether armed or not) to deal with that kind of terror without severe consequences to life, limb or family. Most decent people would rather suffer the consequences than actually organizing and preparing to go to war over it!
So, intimidation, by any means, is a hugely effective way to control people and to achieve dastardly goals. Trump' all 3.

10   What immediately comes to mind is Hitler's Brown Shirts or the early days of the Gestapo. These groups of faux unofficial militias roamed the streets and intimidated Jewish businesses and people, who, having been identified by an informant, were considered to be not loyal to the "Regime". They would then be harassed constantly until they changed their position, were drummed out of their jobs or living quarters or "accidentally killed". As a result, you tend to end up with only "believers" or "informants". Either way, it is the Dictator who wins!

Let's take this 1930's behavior to the present day. When a sane-sounding citizen writes a tweet criticizing the non-Democratic actions of the Destructive party, I can guarantee you that that person will almost immediately start receiving nasty, harassing, threatening phone calls from Florida, South Carolina, Georgia, Texas, Mississippi, etc. etc. that persist for days or weeks. The timing and duration is always closely tied to the timing of the tweet. When those calls are tracked, they quite often come from the same number or a number in a phone bank sequence of numbers. The point is, it is so clear that they are part of a highly organized plan and network that it is easy to track them and turn them over to the DOJ and the FBI for prosecution. This kind of harassment is insidious and extremely disruptive to a well-oiled Democracy. No excuses!

Where this has become so completely serious is when this technique is used to severely intimidate local poll workers in swing states. The national news has given many, many examples of hardworking poll workers who were "run out" of their jobs by this kind of harassment, death threats, personal intimidation and LIES that have been broadcast nationally about them!

DO EVERYTHING that is TOTALLY UNEXPECTED

When the worst pandemic in almost a hundred years visited earth in Wuhan, China in December 2019, the entire world was woefully unprepared. The first reaction was that this was just a really bad flu variant. When China quarantined Wuhan on 1/23l20 by closing businesses and decreeing that all people stay indoors in their homes, it became clear that this was no ordinary flu variant. America was affected by the arrival of tour boat passengers from China arriving at west coast ports. Air traffic from China also became a concern, leading to early quarantine of passengers as they arrived in the US. Mid-January, cases appeared in both Washington and California. February 3, 2020 the US declared a Public Health Emergency. The virus was beginning to spread exponentially - and spread to parts of the rest of the world rapidly in the coming months.

Apparently, our president was not happy about this pandemic coming to the United States - especially just before the next election. As a result, the MAGA GOP started to deny that this virus would be a problem. The President started pronouncing that, like the annual flu, this illness would begin to go away as the weather warmed up in the spring. In fact, he declared that things would be so much better that we should all be able to go to church on Easter Sunday. Since we did not have a vaccine for this illness, it was clear that this virus would expand exponentially to the point of eventually killing a million people in the United States. That message was totally at odds with the strong impression that Trump wanted to leave with his base. He was determined to minimize the adverse effects of this very inconvenient virus upon his prospects for re-election in 2020. Thus, he began the propaganda campaign intended to deny that anything was real about this virus.

12   So, if public health would declare that wearing masks was indicated, the MAGA GOP declared that they would not be enforced in schools or businesses. In other words, they were determined to do just the opposite of what would be common sense and standard practice to save lives on a large scale. This soon became the mantra for almost everything that had been normal in all of our lives. If Democrats said THIS, the GOP would say THAT. If there were laws that were generally accepted by all, the GOP would pass laws to block them or totally reverse them, perhaps for spite, but generally to make the citizens PAY with PAIN or detrimental consequences.

This trend became codified to the point of it being the entire playbook to let all of the citizens know that Governors like DeSantis in Florida or Greg Abbott in Texas were the Bosses and the citizens were clearly the servants. If it makes sense to everyone, make sure that everyone in the state understands that "the Boss" is going to make you live under something that makes absolutely no sense to you. If it used to seem right, pass laws to make what would be the opposite to be the law.

Hey, Buddy, it's the law. Sound anything like the laws that Putin has been passing in Russia to keep all of the citizenry in line in Russia - especially when it comes to his unpopular war against Ukraine? I'm sorry, if you mention the word WAR, you can be sent to jail for 15 years. In Texas, they passed a very unpopular law that banned abortions. However, the law allows vigilantes to enforce the law by taking the apparent offender to court and suing them for $10,000. Sound like the days of yore in the Old West? The bottom line is to punish everyone who doesn't abide by your totally absurd laws - even if it involves punishing major businesses, like Disney or Disney world, that are major sources of revenue for your state. It is apparent that the GOP is no longer interested in serving their constituents!

What in the world would be the most heinous, confusing, baffling thing that a tyrant could do to a God Loving, caring, empathetic, trusting group of people? It would be to do the cruelest, most heinous, terrifying, mind boggling and, yes, just downright Nasty Cruel things to them! Not only would that get their attention very quickly, but it would let them know that their best interests are not at heart. They would know that the tyrant is not at all empathetic or sympathetic. The tyrant might even wear a "I Really, don't Care, DO U?" jacket to visit the forcibly separated kids at the Mexican border. You see, even though we clearly suspected it at the time, we now know that those very cruel brutal separations of small children from their parents or families at the border was the intended cruelty of the plan. Cruelty was fully planned and intended to be the THING! Not only was the brutal separation one of the Cruelest things that the Devil could imagine, they went further to devise a system where these children and parents would never ever be reunited! Cruelty, on a very sinister scale, was the THING!

These anti-abortion laws that were passed in Texas, Florida, Georgia, etc. are so heinous and arcane that the "unintended consequences" that necessarily occur are absolutely the cruelest, inhumane results imaginable. Doctors who would normally be bound by the Hippocratic oath would be put into limbo as to safeguarding lifesaving procedures that normally would be required to be performed without the slightest hesitation. Normal life saving medications would be believed to be banned at the risk of very severe imprisonment, penalties or even death. All of Feminine medicine essentially broke down or totally disintegrated as a direct result of these laws. Even SCOTUS is corrupted to the point that they have

14   become an ORGAN of the heinous, Cruelty is the Thing, party!

Hitler used these very same cruel "separation of Children from their parents" tactics in the rounding up of 6 million Jews and incinerating them in gas furnaces during World War II. To those of us who lived during those times and have extensively read descriptive representations of those terrible years - know all too well - how many insanely CRUEL THINGS were directed at the population that found themselves suddenly at odds with the REGIME due to no fault of their own! CRUELTY was the THING for HITLER as it clearly is for the former Resident of the White House and to his hoard of SYCOPHANTIC DEVIANTS that crawled out from the obscure corners of the UNDERWORLD. Is it any surprise that the thing that happened in Germany in the late 1930's/early 1940's at Hitler's bidding, happened between 2016 and 2020 under the direction of the previous Resident in the White House?

Normal societies are totally incapable of contemplating such things or having to experience them or watching as others are subjected to such dastardly, inhumane tortures and CRUEL behaviors. We just cannot comprehend the excessive cruelty of such heinous acts. We apparently have lived charmed lives under a Democracy far too long to have even an inkling of the breadths and depths of how demonic a previously normal person can go under the mesmeric influences of a personified SATAN! Until it happens directly to you, you are likely to witness these things with total disbelief and try to rationalize them away as hearsay. But when that happens, it's TOO late!

Let's talk about the new order of things in the Republican party. There is this totally asymmetric behavior in elections that "normal" people just do not comprehend and are having a very hard time understanding in order to defend against it to save America. It is this dual level of comprehension that is the very basis of the asymmetric advantage. When one part of the society is running on an entirely different level of the play book, the formerly acceptable level is clearly at a distinct disadvantage. It is like playing football and the other team starts playing with baseball bats and spiked clubs. How do you compete with a sudden rule change, like that, in a game?

Ok, so how does this go? Number one, the goal is to win every election, no matter what the cost or whatever methodology is required to do it. When I say whatever methodology I mean those are the two most operative words in the new Republican party! You have to understand one very fundamental fact, above all else, in their new calculations. They cannot be shamed, disgraced, belittled or embarrassed. The people that they want to elect don't have to know anything, understand anything or believe in anything. They can even be the most despicable people - just as long as they may have some sort of "popular" calling card such as being a celebrity, star football player, or something like that.

Why, you say? How can a total idiot be a Senator or a Congressman and know how to do their job? How do they write laws and make important decisions about the betterment of our citizens' lives if they are totally ignorant? For the GOP, THEY DON'T HAVE to do ANY of THAT. That is the crux and basis of the asymmetric problem. All the GOP wants now is pure power over everyone else and that means they only need a body in the role - a kind of square peg in a round hole - to block every opposition legislation and to rubber stamp every oppressive GOP legislation. All they need is to be totally loyal through an oath to the master (or dictator), to take orders, and to learn how to vote when called to vote the total party line.

16   They are not really there to work for the people or to legislate, but to HOLD POWER to further control through application of TOTAL POWER, as a dictator would do.

Almost any idiot can serve that purpose. Here's the problem for America. There are already a bunch of GOP Congressmen in those offices doing nothing but blowing smoke, making trouble and spreading dissension. I could name dozens of them but for people who understand what I'm talking about, you know them all too well, already. The asymmetry is that Democrats can't get it into their heads that those people are not like they were years ago when many of them took the job seriously. The MAGA GOP don't care about either people or a Democratic America. They only care that they block all of the Democrats' business and "the communist path to destruction" because the GOP are for only one thing and that is winning and progression to a Fascist Authoritarian Dictatorship.

If they have to cheat, they will cheat. If they have to claim the election was stolen, they will claim it was stolen. If they have to lie to win, they will lie. In order to win, if they have to run against everything they did in their recent past, even though it runs counter to their campaign positions, they will deny everything that was part of their past. If they have to be certifiable hypocrites to win, they will do everything that it takes to win. And if all of this is not successful, they will just simply steal the election by force of faux militias, intimidation or passing laws that allow them to entirely ignore the vote.

And, what does the other party do? They try singing ineffective Kumbaya songs, and abiding by Rule of Law and decency. No wonder we say that the Democrats bring soup ladles to street fights because of their belief in the Constitution, Rule of Law and the sanctity of humanity.

They feel that they "must be the adults in the room." Well, my friends, sometimes the consequences of inaction are so totally destructive and life altering that truly drastic measures must be taken to protect the sanctity and the survival of our Democratic way of life. When a hurricane hits Florida, like IAN did weeks ago, it is imperative to immediately put in place extraordinary measures and rules in order to mitigate a totally devastating destruction of lives and property. These are not normal practices or rules, but they are temporarily, absolutely, necessary to apply these rules for the best chance of survival.

The very same thing must be done when Fascist Autocratic tactics, similar to those used by Hitler to take over Germany in the 30's and 40's, are being directed to destroy the United States. Martial Law must be declared and extraordinary use of resources must be used to immediately nip this very real threat in the bud right NOW! Faux militias, for example, are against the law in all 50 states and as well as in the Nation. Every one of them must be rounded up and incarcerated as soon as possible, to prevent their being used as threats before and after the elections in November. They cannot be allowed to intimidate voters now or ever. Besides, intimation with a weapon is a crime on its own merits.

The "chatter" about an impending civil war has drastically increased in these months leading to the elections. We must not have "Brown Shirts" or "Gestapo Units" altering our elections. We are 90% there at this moment and 0% is the only level that is acceptable. Every one of the top 2000 or so Insurrectionists that were either in or were prime designers of the Treasonous Insurrection into the Capitol on 1/6/21 should have been arrested and incarcerated before April of 2021! We have allowed those loose FAD cannons to run amuck to stir up a deadly brew against our Nation for far too long.

18   Martial Law should have been declared to stop this runaway train from creating a deadly train wreck of our Nation as soon as November 8th, 2022! There are 299 "election denier" candidates running for very crucially effective positions in 26 states. These include Congressman, Senators, and Governors but, almost more importantly, Secretaries of States and election certifiers who all have crucial roles in DECIDING the outcome of State and National elections.   If even a few of them get elected, our Democracy is in very dire straits and possibly headed to become a "FAD", a (Fascist Autocratic Dictatorship).

Not only are these new politicians not normal to our Democratic way of life, they cannot be made to be ashamed, embarrassed or intimidated to change their ways. In fact, they are DAMN proud of being this way and of professing these radical ideologies. It is a dramatic part of the Asymmetric War.

As a sidebar at this point in the discussion, I recently saw a movie that had quite a bit to say about this new behavior. The movie itself was disappointing despite the 50's clothing and cars. However, it inadvertently showed, very effectively, much of the sycophantic loyalty to a charismatic, yet Demonic, leader. The movie was called 'Don't worry, Darling.' The leader, who had hired all of these people to work on a highly secret project, was not only charismatic but very controlling! In a dramatic scene, he had promoted a sycophantic follower to a higher position before the entire assemblage of the utopian community. This was done to compel the employee to keep his wife in line with community protocols. She had been beginning to suspect that not everything was kosher in this UTOPIA!

After the 'promotion' the supplicant was made to dance before the entire assemblage in a very dehumanizing and humiliating way. He had to dance not just for a moment but for

a very degradingly long time - much as a puppet on a 19
string would dance or as a monkey on a chain as in the British
term: 'monkey grinder'. (British def. in Collinsdictionary.com)

It was understood from the git go that the Residents in this
Utopia were not allowed to question anything and were
rewarded for this by being supplied with every need to keep
them dumb and happy much as the Romans interests were
modulated during the time of the "Roman Circuses".

While I watched this part of the movie, I could not stop
thinking about the way people like Trump's subservient
disciples behave to snap to his every whim, desire and need.
They are so servile that they even go to extended, contorted
lengths to outdo each other to compete for his attention.
Having seen that poor soul do the 'monkey grinder' dance in
the movie it's hard for me to believe that so many of those
previously reasonable people have willingly subjected
themselves to the role of 'monkey dancing' lackeys for the
narcissistic CLOWN.

How disgustingly humiliating it must be for every one of them!
Have they ever watched themselves "monkey grinder" dance
on the chain of this Devilish Con Man? You can name them all.
Graham Cracker, Southern Cotton, Yellow Meadows, The Red
Ruby, Down the Halley, Cancun Cruz, Charlie McCarthy, River
Jordan, Great Scott, Burn baby Burn, Not so Blunt, Not so
Newness, The big Johnson, The a-Pauling, etc. – each one
digging deeper than the rest and especially deep for the
MONKEY GRINDER! A dangerous sign for our times! The
Criminal Leader and his "secrets" were highly guarded by
armed militias such as The Oath Keepers or The Proud Boys!

CHAPTER 6
The Effect of the NORMALIZATION of LIES

This chapter disturbs me so very much to write. But, far more devastating to me, and especially for America, is the terrible effect that it has on the prospects for even a slight chance of survival from the Horrific effects that it has upon our Future.

After following those horrid details since 2014, I had a sudden epiphany that we were orders of magnitude worse off than what had normally been considered as the destruction of our Democracy to date. I mean 100's to 1000's of times worse than the normal revelations that have been uncovered to this point by the Jan 6th committee or by other facts revealed in recent books from some "near insiders" to the 45th administration.

So many people, throughout his 4 yr. term, assumed that all of his bad or weird behavior was the result of his personality, his narcissism, or just his bad manners and egotism. As we are finding out, drip by drip, what was actually going on from day one was a very detailed and completely involved plan to totally destroy America and its Democracy and to generate, instead, a Fascist Authoritarian Dictatorship (FAD). His apparent "bumbling and ineptness" was just part of his 'shtick' to cover.

When we begin to see what detail was actually involved - so cleverly hidden - we see that this bumbling fool (who could rarely put together a coherent sentence) was involved in intricate, complicated, destructive schemes that were far, far-above his capabilities. Therefore, he was relying upon much more advanced and deviant sources such as from the high-level Think Tanks of the Soviet Union. These people, as well as their august leader, Putin, must have studied every loophole, nook and cranny of our Constitution and institutions.

As a result, we are just beginning to see through the fog into the vast range and scope of this monstrous plot to totally destroy America. It's not as if we have not been adequately forewarned by perceptive political scientists that saw warnings of planned disasters as derived from the history of Hitler's rise to power when he destroyed the Democracy of Germany in the 30's and 40's. (There were considerable forewarnings of these monstrous connections, plots and schemes in books published two and three years ago that totally forewarned of these impending disasters with sufficient lead time to take swift and decisive action to mitigate the consequences before they got close to certain disaster.) See AMERICA DIES WHEN BASED UPON LIES and PUTIN'S PUPPET or THE TERRIBLE TURD in the PALATIAL PUNCHBOWL. (Amazon press, 2020 and 2021 respectively).

Many of us lived through the rise to power of Adolf Hitler and the resulting WWII that devastated so many people around the world and yet was only a trifling compared to the 6 million Jews that were eliminated in the Holocaust. There have been so many books and movies about those times and draconian tactics that no educated person should be ignorant of those monstrous events and means to destruction. Every person in these United States should be well-versed by now of those horrible tactics, deceits, and manipulations that allowed Germany and then all of Europe to fall under that terrible scourge from the THIRD REICH. Every one of us should have recognized, if not early, then certainly after January 6, that this "would be Hitler" was well rooted to power within our midst!

The big question, now, is what extraordinary things and planning are we prepared to do to rid America of this CANCER including the considerable entourage and camp followers that are working every second of every hour 24/7 to totally destroy

22 our Beautiful America. Based upon the total lack of action of our Justice Department over the past almost two years - the answer seems to be, absolutely almost nothing. Anyone who has studied how Hitler took over Germany would understand one very important fact: There is NO NEGOTIATING with TERRORISTS! There's no shaming, embarrassing or reasoning with them. They have a plan, a mantra, a goal, a determination to succeed at whatever Destructive plan that they have set their minds to and have taken a solemn pledge to finish it. If something doesn't work, they will plan and try three more until they succeed. I.e., they are not normal politicians and have absolutely no intention of ever being normal people! It is as if zombies have invaded their beings and are driving their every step. They are single minded and no amount of Kumbaya, bull shit, or persuasion is going to change their course. It seems that only jail time will help.

So how do you deal with this way of life that is hell bent upon destroying American Democracy? There is only one action that they understand or that can deter them. It is slamming their asses in jail as soon and as deliberately as possible and with absolutely the longest penalty time allowed. PERIOD! That is all that they understand or respond to. To do otherwise tells them that they have lived for another day to plan and to spew hate and destruction. Those who entered the Capitol on January 6th all committed Treason against the United States or at the very least they committed Insurrection against the US, which is a Federal Crime spelled out in the Constitution. Doing anything less is considered to be a sign of weakness that gives them more strength and solidarity.

There is a fundamental truth that you may have picked up on in these last two paragraphs. The slow acting Rule of Law may seem a bit abused here. Let me tell you right here and now, dealing with Terrorists whether foreign or domestic, isn't a normal process and demands extraordinary procedures and processes which can be done while still maintaining a modicum of attention to humanity and Rule of Law processes.

Ask anyone who lived in Germany in the late 30's and early 40's and they would tell you, without any hesitation, that they wish that the German government had dealt with the Gestapo and the Brown Shirts very early and decisively when it was clear that they could lead to the nation's downfall in just a few years. They would also say that they wished that someone would have done something about the courts very quickly when it was clear that they were being corrupted. They would also say that something should be done about the taking over of news organizations and operation of the propaganda sites.

The thing about all of this boils down to the concept of asymmetric warfare. When you are dealing with people who are committed to taking down your 246-year-old Democracy by any and every means possible, you are not dealing with a democratic process or anyone rational. If they need to lie constantly to tear down trust - THEY WILL LIE. If they need to threaten violence, they'll THREATEN VIOLENCE. If they need to corrupt every court in the land, they WILL CORRUPT EVERY COURT IN THE LAND! If they need to set up and run propaganda organs, they WILL SET UP AND RUN the PROPAGANDA ORGANS! If they need to stop normal voting and allow cronies to change the outcome of every vote to keep them in power, they WILL CHANGE THE OUTCOME OF EVERY ELECTION NEEDED TO MAINTAIN POWER! If they need to corrupt every law enforcement agency including the FBI, CIA and the military, they will CORRUPT EVERY AGENCY - including the MILITARY! If they will turn every law upside down to torment and terrorize the population, they WILL TURN

24 EVERY LAW UPSIDE DOWN! They are not going to follow any Rule or Law!

Don't you all get it? The game is almost over because they have been successful at doing all of these things, and dozens more, already. The basis of my epiphany about how bad this multipronged onslaught to take down America has become seems to be the result of the total neglect on the part of the Government to take swift and decisive action to cut out this CANCER before it was able to metastasize throughout our society.

All these years of lying, cheating, and demeaning our national institutions and traditions has had a very profound effect upon all of our psyches. The destruction of everything that we used to believe in has been normalized to the extent that we no longer know how to react to small detrimental changes in the world surrounding us until it is far too late. Creeping changes become easily tolerated as a result of this slow onslaught on our tolerance of less than normal behaviors. In politics, this is sometimes called Incrementalism or Gradualism. For a Terrorist, it's a profoundly effective means to disrupt the normal order and business of life in a way that the general public is not able to discern the real danger or risk of these, only slightly, annoying events. As a result, out of confusion, disorientation or just inattention, we are numbed into a trance of non-resistance and passive tolerance. "When they took away the rights of teachers, I was not a teacher so I did nothing." "When they took away the rights of policemen, I was not a policeman so I did nothing." "When they took away the rights of scientists, I was a scientist but by then it was too late." "The game was over and the nation had been lost."

If It's So Bad, WHY ISN'T IT 90% to 10%?

We are two weeks from November 8th, 2022 and the most important midterm election in our entire history as a nation. The outcome of this election, if it goes for the MAGA GOP instead of the Democrats, essentially means the absolute end of our Democracy and we will become a Fascist Autocratic State (FAD) for the foreseeable future. Thus, it would probably be longer than any of our lifetimes. It is that monumental!

Think about it. There are 291 candidates in 40 states that don't believe Biden was elected in 2020 and/or that they will only accept the result of this 2022 election if they win. They openly swear that they will change the outcome if it appears that they have lost. How can that be true? Something drastically wrong must have happened to not just these 291 people running but the millions that would even consider voting for them. That, by itself, is astoundingly insane, but it is so much worse than that. The implications for Democracy are absolutely devastating! Would you believe that many of these candidates are ignorant, illiterate, unschooled celebrities? They have a zero record at legislating and have no concern for the wellbeing of the constituents that they represent. They are only subservient sycophants to the HERR Leader.

How did we get to this despicable place in late 2022? How could so many people totally lose every sense of what makes the very essence of their lives, if not a land of opportunity and success, then, at least, bearable without HARASSMENT from the government? I'm reminded of a book I was required to read in a sociology class in college: Escape from Freedom by Erich Fromm, Farrar @ Rinehart publisher in 1941. God, how many years ago was that? Of course it seemed like a waste of

26   times during those years. Life was abundant and the football games were great and the dating – Ooh La La - the Dating - (just now an Italian gesture with the hand) - OH, THE DATING! It seemed like everyone had two cars, two houses - one at the beach or one high in the mountain's deep rich forest. Perhaps, even two wives, but ah, I do digress. Yes, there was a lot of that going around as well. Times since have generally been good and prosperous so why would we need to Escape from Freedom? Hell if I know why. That good life must have affected quite a few or we wouldn't be at this demise!

So, what did that seemingly out of place and time book have to say? It said that when we have Freedom we may feel at odds of knowing exactly what to do. With freedom we may feel very decidedly alone and not supported by others. Laws and Order provide us a kind of condition of not only belonging but also gives us a sense of support, a "stiffening" structure, that supports us and keeps us contained, focused and directed. A breakdown of Law-and-Order leaves us with a very uneasy feeling that things may be going wrong without our being able to correct them. That leaves us with an absurdly disturbing feeling of hopelessness. To deliberately break down the norms of Law and Order is a sure-fire way to totally disorient a society, and thereby, is a way to destroy an entire Democracy.

Isn't it ironic that we were required to read the book during the best of times - many decades before the meaning became so much clearer in this terrible age. Perhaps, the reading of the book then, allowed me and others to fully predict, 2, 3 or more years ago, where this Maniacal Monster was taking this totally Woebegone naive population, that had lived the highlife that they must have thought would last forever, to the very hell of a Hitler's Germany in the 40's, or Putin's maniacal destruction of a beautiful people and a nation in the Ukraine or to a Kim

Jong-Un ruled over a subservient, marshaled horde of desperate souls in North Korea.

HISTORY MATTERS! The rise of Mussolini's Fascism in Italy in the 30's MATTERS! The rise of Hitler's Nazism in Germany in the 30's/40's MATTERS! The marching of White Supremacist groups in Charlottesville, Va. on 8/11/2017 MATTERS! The appointment of three Ultra-Right, White judges from the Federalist Society to the Supreme Court in 2018/2020 MATTERS! The weaponization of the Justice Department and making the AG your personal defender and henchman, MATTERS! Using the IRS to audit the taxes of your enemies and opponents, MATTERS! The attempt to totally destroy NATO MATTERS! The cozy trips to speak privately with Kim Jung-Un, MATTER! The many direct conversations with Putin, that were not supervised or recorded, in person and by phone, MATTER! Thirty thousand deliberate LIES in 4 years, MATTER! Hundreds of direct contacts with 200+ high level operatives around the Kremlin during the 2016 campaign, MATTER! The Treasonous attempt to overthrow the US Government by force on 1/6/21, MATTERS!

Why didn't we see this coming? Why did it take the news media until just a week or so ago to begin to see what was staring them in the face for the past 4 years? Why didn't the Democratic party have meetings every day for the past 3 years planning out countermeasures to avert this pending disaster? Kumbaya just does not cut it with terrorists and traitors! There should have been decisions made, immediately, about what to do with all election deniers and all future planned MAGA GOP actions before the November 8, 2022 election. The MAGA GOP have been meeting 24/7 for years to plan all of the ways that they would be taking to permanently alter the basis of our societal mores and lifestyles. Where were we all of that time?

Again?! Why did 135 Million People BUY the LIE?

Even if you didn't know anything about what happened to Germany in the 40's, you have very definitive examples of how bad it is to live in N Korea under the iron thumb of Kim Jung-Un and now in the Ukraine or Russia under the Demonic Rule of a true Monster - Putin. It has to be pure hell to even try to survive under those extreme, autocratic dictatorship regimes. Yes, I know, none of us have lived there and experienced it directly, but there is a plethora of remotely observed conditions that would raise hairs up your neck and send chills screaming through your body. Almost everyone in today's world would have a pretty good feel for how bad it would be to be a common resident of those horrid places. Think of everything that you enjoy in life here and now and just KISS IT GOODBYE. That is how it would be for a change from a Democracy to a Fascist Autocratic Dictatorship. I don't know why anyone would wish that for themselves!

Oh, now I see it. It's the difference between being a resident or citizen or being the dictator himself. Are you looking at the situation as the one oppressed or as the one in power that is doing the oppression? I have a very important clue for all of you "would be dictators:' in any autocratic country THERE IS ONLY ONE DICTATOR! EVERYONE ELSE is subservient to that dictator. EVERYONE ELSE - no exceptions! So, the 200 or so in the house and senate or the 185 million who are buying this BIG LIE nonsense - where will you all be in this pyramid scheme that has only one person in power at the top?! Dead, in jail or excommunicated, period! Think about that a bit. How much fun do you think you and your family will be having after a Narcissistic CLOWN is elected SUPREME RULER of all of you? I don't think that it will be very pleasant!

For some very obscure reason, the people that held seats in our Congress to enact effective legislation for the benefit of their constituents, NOW, don't care about anything but holding absolute power over everyone living in the Nation. That means that they have no legislative agenda because they don't intend to ever have to run for office. They don't care about those people that they were formerly supposed to serve. Their idea of an election now is I win no matter how the vote comes out. When any politician feels that way, they have absolutely no reason to ever be beholden to any constituent. They simply don't need them anymore, except as a source of tax money that the politicians can spend any way they feel like, because the people can no longer vote them out of office. At this point we no longer have a Democracy! You might as well live in N Korea or Russia because you no longer have any rights or a say in the matter. WE ARE 95% THERE NOW! VERY SAD!

Again, I can begin to see why politicians might feel a benefit in declaring that all elections in the future will be called out as being corrupt or fraudulent. This allows them to contest them and monkey with the results to the point that they always win. But, why in the world would voters deliberately vote for people that have stated that they will declare their votes to be null and void? I would think knowing that someone was clearly going to cheat them out of their vote, and thus their only influence, would be something that they would vote against? Come to think of it, that is kind of an oxymoron. You exercise your sovereign right to vote with intense knowledge that you are going to destroy that right forever. It just doesn't make any sense! It's like handing a person a loaded gun and telling them to shoot themselves. And guess what, they do it ever so willingly! It reminds me of the fable about the "Pied Piper" who played his tune and marched all of the children off to oblivion. People under the spell of Demons WILL drink the KOOL AID!

30   OK, that can't be all of it. I cannot believe that everyone that crawls out from under a rock can be that IGNERT, that STUPID or that mesmerized over the charisma of a LOSER, reality TV show star. Yes, it's true that anyone that buys into the many conspiracy theories, such as QAnon who actually believes this garbage, is truly Ignorant enough (I mean gullible enough) to act upon those beliefs and to do damage to others. Those people were just born that way and they are the victims of their own circumstances. We must pity them because they are just incapable of having a modicum of sanity or reason and simply are not capable of Critical Thinking.

However, there are those 200 or more politicians in the House and Senate that espouse the big LIE that the 2020 election was stolen from '45' by Biden and those devil inspired, Communist Democrats. There are also other 'so called educated' people throughout the country that espouse the BIG LIE. There are many Governors in red states, many slack attorneys and nouveau riche industrialists like the "Pillow Man" or "the Rocket Man" as well as Ginni Thomas. It really should be clear to everyone by now that they all know that the "BIG LIE" is actually false – a figment of someone's imagination. It was a deliberately planned and executed devilish contrivance to destroy all truth and faith in the temple of Democracy; the universal vote and peaceful transition of power or the Golden BASIS for maintaining a Democracy. Instead of it being a stupid belief in a demonstrable LIE, it is a scheme - possibly planned by Russian Think Tanks - to destroy a proud Shining City on the Hill of Democracy - the United States of America. The so-called educated Media have been fooled for more than three years about whether this is something that these people actually believe. It is part of a long-term plan and is being executed flawlessly by these "actors". It is the major thrust of this election and is about to work flawlessly! SADLY, that is TRUE!

WHY is it Always the WORDS that MATTER?

How many times must I say this? The MAGA GOP isn't hiding anything now, nor have they been for three years. Actually, for many of us who have studied the history of the rise of Tyrants (a word related to Tyranny as in <u>Oh, Tyranny</u> a book to be published in December, 2022) - such as the rise of Hitler in Germany, Mussolini in Italy, Putin in Russia or Kim Jung-Un in N. Korea - have all known since 2015, when Trump came down the escalator and talked about foreigners polluting our society with rapists, drugs and crime, what he was actually intending to do with America. And, as one who studies such histories, <u>it</u> can be known by the <u>Five Steps to Tyranny</u>. (Jason Kottke of Kottke.org Nov. 23, 2016 or Bartleby.com/essay) 1. "Us" and "Them" (prejudice and the formation of a dominant group). 2. "Obey Orders" (the tendency to follow orders, especially from those of authority). 3. Do "them" harm (obeying an authority who commands actions against our conscience). 4. "Stand up" or "Stand by" (standing by as harm occurs). 5. "Exterminate" (the elimination of the "other").

Ok, to every voter about to vote in the polls next week, the knowledge of those <u>Five Steps to Tyranny</u> should be words that would not only raise the hairs up your necks, but send shuddering chills to the tip of your toes! Even if you didn't know anything about those multiple documented steps, at least you have surely seen what overtly happened on 1/6/2021! Even if you were loyal to him and had no doubts before, what happened in the Capitol on that day should have shaken every American right down to the core! That is because, before, most people could easily rationalize it as a deviation of character. Jan 6, 2021 could not be explained by deviation - it was a full blown, for everyone to see, real deal. FULL STOP!

32   However, isn't it very interesting that almost every man (or woman) that was in the Capitol on 1/6/21 and for a few days after, condemned what happened then in no uncertain terms - GOP or Democrat alike - it made no difference. But just a few days later, one by one, the GOP members crept back to the dictator and "kissed his ring" (could've been anything other than his ring) and pledged renewed allegiance to Herr Fuhrer!

Obviously, one of the surest signs that a dictator is in power is when bootlickers pledge loyalty oaths to him rather than to the defense of the Constitution or of the Rule of Law. Out of 300 or so Congressmen, there were only 2 or 3 that didn't creep back into the fold of Monkey Grinders. (English term for a lackey who dances like an obedient Monkey at the end of a chain controlled by the Organ Grinder Master). How pathetic is a vision of a person like the Graham Cracker dancing like a GD fool on the end of that chain like a lowly, forcibly humiliated animal such as the Organ Grinder's Monkey?! Don't they know how they look? Every one of them must feel like a lowly circus animal begging for treats from the animal master. Don't they all know by now that there can be only one animal master in the circus? And don't they know by now that they aren't, nor will they ever be, that animal master? They are so very SAD!

Ah, but I digress for a moment. The point is that the whole world knew after 1/6/21 who Der Fuhrer was and what he had been up to since probably 2013 when he was near Moscow at a Miss Universe Pageant. Every one of those Grinder Monkeys knows that everything they are doing and espouse to their constituents is a LIE - in fact it is a very BIG LIE! Now they don't even hide that fact anymore. They are making demands that all "endorsed Republicans" that are running must be ELECTION DENIERS, and state that they are election deniers. Every American should know what that means to their future!

Either you are for Democracy or you are for a dictator that will ensure that you will never have a vote ever again. It cannot be both. It is either that you are able to select the people that you want to represent your needs to the Government, and that happens peacefully and smoothly, or you have ZERO rights and absolutely no say in what horrendous things that the government can and will do to you, your families, your children, grandchildren and far beyond! Stop and think about that premise for just a moment! Think very hard about what that truly means. Let it sink in for a while. By voting for ANY REPUBLICAN EVER AGAIN, YOU are THROWING AWAY your ENTIRE LIFE, JOYS and FREEDOMS! Essentially, that one vote will do that forever. Essentially, that would be for the rest of your lives and those of your children.

Why is anyone even considering voting for these charlatan Monkey Grinders ever again if all of this is so obvious and readily recognizable since the GOP has been telling you this for almost two years now? I mean, look at the scum they dragged up for you to consider voting for. An ex-football player that can't even put a sentence together. A wife beater and a person that would have a girlfriend have an abortion even though he claims to not believe in abortions. A snake oil doctor who has been on TV and doesn't even live in the state that he is pretending to represent. A person that originally was an outspoken Trump Denier and now is endorsed by Trump. What a total hypocrite! A person in a cowboy hat that was part of the Bundy group that claimed none of the land they were using for grazing belonged to a legitimate government. An ex-TV star that claims that the 2020 election was stolen and that no election in the future will be ever won by anyone other than approved Republicans. All of them believe in voter intimidation and voter suppression. They believe that all elections will be decided by force or by guns!

CHAPTER 10
101 Marketing, Parables, TALL TALES and the BIG LIE

So, we all now know exactly what the MAGA GOP will do if they are elected to be in charge of the House or Senate or, heaven forbid, both Houses. As they have already shown us in Florida and Texas, they are hell-bent on drafting and enacting horrific, insanely cruel laws that they will enforce with either severe monetary penalties or outrageous times in jail. The law against abortion has been devilishly constructed so that the State itself is not the enforcer, but that it is left up to citizen vigilantes to find, take to court, and sue offenders for $10,000 or more. What a fiendish law! It sets citizen against citizen and makes it very lucrative for ordinary people to go after their neighbors and perhaps even friends or family. Oh, my God, has no one read anything about life in Germany under Hitler or what it was like in Russia under Stalin and now under Putin?

People who did not believe in Nazism tried in vain to just live their lives as best they could without any hassle. However, when at work, church or a social meeting place, it was soon made very clear that you were not welcome unless you joined the Nazi party. Worse yet, not only would you have to bear up under the constant harassment of not being welcome, but soon you would be made to feel that you had actually been excommunicated, as used to happen in some religious communities. If at work, you would eventually be fired from your job and it would soon be clear that no other company would hire you after that sudden expulsion from your only means of a living. Oh, did you all miss that day in class when ostracization from your life was covered? Sorry that you missed that day in class. Perhaps you should have at least read your assigned reading list so you would have known how your life might suddenly turn out if you hadn't joined!

See, all of us, including those in the news media, have $\qquad$
not ever lived in a place like Hitler's Nazi Germany or Putin's Russia! We all still think that people are like our friends, our loved ones and, yes, even our former politicians who represented us in OUR Government. They may have been shady, not quite above board or out to make a buck on the side, but in general they were there to get things done for the betterment of the country. Most of us have never actually met truly despicably evil people! Most have not met people that do not care about our lives any more than they would in killing an ant or a mosquito. There is only one life of meaning to them - their own! Power is everything. Overwhelming force is everything. Cruelty is everything. Totally Asymmetrical warfare is everything to them. There are no rules to be followed or obeyed. All traditions are to be nullified and destroyed. All order is to be overturned as was done to the money tables in the biblical temple. There's absolutely nothing normal here.

As I have said before and I absolutely emphasize it now; there is no negotiating with these kinds of TERRORISTS! The only thing that they understand is being thrown in jail and the key being thrown away! Even then, they may believe that to be a temporary inconvenience if their kind are left to get them out. Look at Putin! He started a totally asymmetrical war against the peaceful Ukrainians. Even if he gets his entire army destroyed - every last tank, truck and missile destroyed - he will never admit that he did anything wrong unless he is somehow executed by his own military or a national tribunal. I guarantee to you that he will not face the consequences of the war crimes that he has committed against the humanity of the peace-loving Ukrainian Nation. A more-sane man might have cut his losses and tried to make some lame excuse that others had kept him from obtaining his goals of total destruction and acquiescence of the territory and people of that nation. Him?

36   Again, how many times does it have to be said. These people, these MAGA GOP freaks, have already told you and showed you many times how it will turn out for every one of you if you vote to get them elected. They have even told you long in advance, that even if you think that you have voted them out they will never accept that outcome. If it must come to the January 6th, 2022 type of force, intimidation and deadly threat, they have already prepared and trained the armies to do that for them. Have you not heard of the Proud Boys, the Three Percenters, the Boogaloo Boys, the Oath Keepers? Oh, no? Have you ever heard of the Gestapo or the Brown Shirts in Nazi Germany or the Black shirts (Italian Camicia Nera) in Mussolini's Fascist Italy? Oh, no? You will get to know them!

Well, you had better get prepared for them because they are coming to a voting booth near you and after the election they will probably be called in to assist the enforcement of the ill-gotten outcome of the midterm elections. Of course, election fraud will be claimed and a little public persuasion might just have to be called in to make the claim stick. Friends, in your naive state, YOU HAVE NOT SEEN ANYTHING YET! After November 8th, if it doesn't go the way the MAGA GOP think it should go, I'll wager that you will see plenty of violence that none of you have ever thought about before. These boys in Idaho are already talking about being ready for the racial civil war. Probably, based upon what the experts are hearing on the internet, every other faux militia group is also talking about a military civil war to take back the "Nation" from the communist liberals. It is puzzling, when faux militias are against the law in all 50 states and the Federal government, why are they not either corralled and locked up or at the very least required to declare every member and a list of every weapon and be regulated by reporting boards as to their activities and planned excursions? This is how Germany fell to the Nazis!!

Oh, I'm sorry if you thought that this part of the story was over. There just happens to be much more that is pertinent to how your life will be totally changed - as if you now lived in a black hole of HELL after the election. Guess what, one of the most sinister things that will happen to you is that you will no longer be secure in knowing who you are talking to and what might happen to you or your family if you might say something to a "close friend" that just happens to "rat on you" to people who will do harm to you or your family. You now find yourself in that terrible condition of not knowing whom you can trust. You see, your best friend at work or church may have been either asked to or coerced to spy on you and your friends and acquaintances. Everyone loyal to the "STATE" will be assigned the task of reporting to the authorities everything that they hear or see that they may find as being suspicious in your behavior or your contacts.

Think about that for a very long time now! Can you imagine what that is going to do almost immediately to your social life? Who knows, that spy may even be your wife, daughter or son. Think about that! What in hell is that going to do to your family life? Do you now understand what kind of hell it will be when you absolutely cannot trust anyone ever again? Oh, yes, sending someone a suggestive email about how to take action to resist? Forget about it! That is a sure-fire way to just one day disappear without a trace. NO FREEDOM WHATSOEVER!

Ok, so you think this is a bit too far. No one is going to do that kind of thing here. For God's sake, this is America. We don't do that kind of thing here. Let me tell you something. It has already started here and has been operating in its early form for at least 4 or 5 years. When I write a tweet that, for whatever reason, rankles some person, I get phone calls from Texas, N Carolina, Florida, Louisiana, Georgia, Michigan and Iowa,

38   as well as from rural areas of my local state. Since I do not answer these calls, they never leave a message. However, I know that other people who answer get terrible threats and get significant harassment from these callers. The numbers, as recorded, are very often the same, or at least from the same bank of numbers, as if they were from an organized call center.

Yes, my friends, you all have been living the good life far too long to even conceive of all of this having been planned and executed for so many years while we all sang KUMBAYA, hoping that a 2020 midterm election would magically stop this FASCIST CANCER DEAD in its TRACKS! Ah, but we were too preoccupied with "stories" about rising crime and inflation.

Hell no, it will not put an end to any of this, because we have looked the other way too long. It has become completely metastasized in our lives for far too long without the drastic measures that would have been required to curtail all of this at least two years ago. Where in Hell was Merrick Garland and the Justice Department when they needed to spring into action immediately after 1/6/21? The only way to defeat this kind of Tyranny is to CUT it OUT immediately and lock them up for a very long time. Ask any German that lived there in the 30's/40's and they will tell you the signs were there very early but the government did nothing to stop the Brown Shirts or the Gestapo when there was still time to nip it in the bud. Then, to their horror, they found out it was too late to do anything but try to survive with it. The iron grip of Tyranny was too tight around the society. The Resistance movement tried but was no match for the SS and the weaponized Gestapo. Even if we magically manage to keep the House and at least 50/50 in the Senate, almost all of the damage has already been done as the Fascist norms are already operating in multiple states such as Florida and Texas.

Oh, Why Didn't I PAY ATTENTION to HISTORY?

After that last chapter, when I re-read it, I was shaken to my very core because it is so ghastly, gruesomely scary to even contemplate that such things could happen to people right here in the United States - the shining beacon upon the hill of Democracy! That just can't be true! Americans don't think that way about other Americans. What kind of people would treat other people with such lack of compassion or contempt for humanity? We are predominantly a religious nation; most world religions teach love for people and caring and sympathy for another's plight. It just cannot be possible.

Well, let me give you a current example of how far down this very dark rabbit hole a large block of Americans has already fallen! Last Friday, a man filled with conspiracy theories and presumably with the GOP MAGA rhetoric about how evil the Democrats are, took it upon himself to break into Nancy Pelosi's home in San Francisco and used a hammer to crack the skull of Mr. Pelosi at 3 in the morning. Fortunately, Nancy was not there. Also fortunately, Mr. Pelosi had been able to call 911 for the police to get there just in time to see the man hit Mr. Pelosi with the hammer. They were able to stop him and arrest him before further damage occurred. Mr. Pelosi certainly would have been killed had the police not arrived when they did.

Ok, one life miraculously saved by a very fortunate sequence of events. The world sent gracious well-wishes and prayers for his rapid recovery and for the two of them for continued good health. Would you believe that in the midst of this very real near- death tragedy that prominent members of the MAGA Influenced world started conspiracy theories about what happened instead

40   of what actually very nearly happened. There were Election Denier candidates that actually made sick jokes to campaign followers about this near-death experience of the Pelosi's that were met with waves of laughter. Prominent business people that are in charge of giant media venues, used that media to spread disgusting falsehoods about the crime. How low can people go? How far have we already gone?

Ok, now what do you say about the compassion and sense of humanity of some of these MAGA GOP people that have already planned for the total destruction of our beloved time-tested Democracy? They have clearly stated that if they get back into power after this election, they will take away everything that good politicians have provided for America over the past 60 years: Social Security, Medicare, ACA, Women's Rights, and women being able to make their own medical decisions, instead of some white men in Congress. They've already censored the curricula and books in schools. Now here's the big one! They are and will make it so you are either restricted from voting, or your vote will simply be thrown out and not counted. There will be laws that allow the partisan legislature to simply override all of the votes! They've already passed laws in States that restrict what you can say, read, see or do. These are no better than laws passed in Russia that fine you and throw you in jail if you use the word "WAR", because they don't want to admit that they have started an illegal war against the peaceful Nation of Ukraine.

So much of this planned cruelty and lack of concern for human values or humanity was evident throughout the rise of Hitler's power in the 30's/40's. Had you all paid attention in your history classes, you would have seen these signs in America years ago when we could have called it out and taken action. Some of us did see it and called it out, but unfortunately, to no avail!

THERE is a SCIENCE Called "SUDDEN THEORY"

What is "Sudden Theory" and what difference does it make from what we have been discussing already in this book? Let's start out with the premise that your life is and has been going very well for a really long time. You are well employed and making a more than adequate income. You happen to be single and life has been good to you in the area of dating and socialization. You are invited to great parties, see good movies, enjoy concerts and appreciate a great play once in a while. You might be married with a great family and everything above is also true for you. It is as if you are living on a line on a graph that is constantly going up. Everything under that line represents good times and great experiences.

One day you are driving to a special event and another car suddenly shoots out from a cross street and T-Bones you in the middle of your driver's side door. That is the moment that your lifeline suddenly, in a microsecond, crosses another line called the disaster event line. Everything below that line was fabulous, but in that microsecond everything above that line is a total nightmare! Your life and every aspect of it has been essentially destroyed - especially if you survive the accident.

Now think of this "Sudden Theory" scenario happening on or about November 8th, 2022 - voting day. One microsecond is all that it takes for essentially that same sort of thing to happen to you, and, ironically, for everyone else in America as well. What kind of Russian Roulette (Pun intended) are we all playing in every election that has occurred in the past decade? Would we bet our houses and jobs on the result of the Super Bowl every year? No, we wouldn't, so why do we do it here?

42   By the way, this cannot be interpreted as a reason to give up voting and counting the votes very accurately (something that has been done in America for at least the past 80 years). No, it is actually a reason for keeping America responsive by having reliable and very accurate elections. That is the only way to keep our servants in government above-board and working for us rather than for huge greedy interests.

No, the point is, in a microsecond, our lives may change for the worst times in our history - save for the Civil War. That is why it is so GD important for everyone in America to visualize the consequences of voting for the MAGA GOP that only wants America to be a Fascist Autocratic Dictatorship! If they win this election, you will definitely be kissing your life goodbye like in this "Sudden Theory" graphic. In a scenario like this, inflation doesn't matter, crime doesn't matter, even abortion doesn't matter because - nothing will ever matter again after an election if the MAGA GOP Election Deniers win!

What kind of person would plan and be delighted to watch, for hours, an armed and deadly Treasonous Insurrection - directed at the US Capitol on 1/6/21? What kind of a person would find glory in a fierce riot that killed 5 and injured 120 policemen? What kind of a person would send a medieval MOB to attack police with bear spray, fire extinguishers, flag poles and clubs, while threatening to kill perhaps 300 Congress members? What kind of person would delight in having his own Vice- President hung in front of his family? What kind of person would LIE to you over 30,000 times in four years (21 times per day) and be proud of it? What kind of person could you trust that LIED to YOU 21 times every day? A President of the United States? Really? No, Really?! By now, it shouldn't surprise you, but we still can't believe it. That is not OUR America and we must not allow it to be so!

Every one of us must ask ourselves these questions.
How can you exist in a world where you absolutely can't trust anything or anyone? How can you live in a world where you can't pray to your own God in your own way? How can you live where you are told everything that you can or can't do or enjoy? How can you live where all of your decisions are made for you and enforced by the Gestapo? How can you live where you are not allowed to protect your children from harm or disease? How can you live in a world where your life or that of your family doesn't matter? What would it mean to you if strangers called you and threatened your family's lives? What would it mean if you were threatened on your way to work by strangers with weapons? How would you feel if, after waiting in line for six hours, your vote was totally destroyed? How would you feel if your house was burned to the ground during the night while you slept? How would you feel if a mob destroyed your business and there was absolutely no recourse? How would you feel if it was decreed that your children will be taken away from you and there is no recourse?

How would you feel if you were required to pay a $10,000 bounty to someone when you bought a gun, for example? How would you feel if strangers with guns stood over you while you voted? How would you feel if your favorite books, movies or concerts were banned, destroyed or burned? How would you feel if everything that you previously loved to do became against the law and you could be put in jail or hung for it? How much would you be longing for what you've known your entire life but is impossible to ever get back? It is gone forever! Well, you are just now beginning to get about 1/10 of the distress you would be in under a Fascist Authoritarian Dictatorship (FAD) run by a person that we have previously known as the President. God help us all before it is all just GD too late to go back to our present life like before November 8th, 2022, for example. Now, do you begin to GET IT?

44   So, for four years we thought that this was essentially just one person, the former Resident of the White House, and a few friends or MONKEY GRINDER hangers-on sycophants. Now we are just a week from the 2022 mid-term election on 11/8/22 and we are confronted with at least 300 ELECTION DENIER candidates that are running for key offices in over 26 states. In addition, we are now dealing with thousands of MAGA GOP voters who have been hornswoggled into believing that the 2020 election was stolen and that they need to make that right again by getting their rightwing Christian (God, I'm about to vomit over that one) savior back into office. Have they ever actually asked themselves what did he ever do for them to make their lives better enough to go to war for him? I doubt that they have an answer for that one, even though they will swear that he did many things for them. Hey, name just one! Will you do that for me? JUST NAME ONE, OK?

What he does have are many faux militia groups, like the Proud Boys, The Three Percenters, the Oath Keepers or the Boogaloos, that are committed to him. They are for him because they have been White Supremacists for many years and he has given them a sense of belonging, authentication and authority. That is much like the Brow Shirts and the Gestapo that were loyal to Hitler during his rise to power in Germany in the 1930's. I know that it has been 90 years, but GOD help us, who in their right minds would go to war for a person whose only goal is clearly to totally destroy their lives and livelihood? For God's sake, people, read just a chapter or two about what your life will be like when the CANCER takes hold in this once beautiful Nation and in your very happy lives!

There are just not enough terrible words in our English language to adequately describe how completely ghastly his Fascist rule will totally destroy all of your lives! FINI, CAPUT!

Spin DISTRUST for Everything – I Mean EVERYTHING!

I know that this may seem to be old fashioned, but do any of you remember, not that long ago, that lying was considered, by almost everyone, as being disqualifying? I know that when I applied for jobs that knowledge that you lied on your resume would end an interview. And being caught lying at work would be certain grounds for being fired - and perhaps even black listed for other jobs. Everyone considered being honest to be an absolute requirement for everything in life.

So, a President comes along that is lying almost every time he opens his mouth. By actual count, 30,000+ LIES in four years in office. That is 21 LIES a day. In the past, had that been the case, people very quickly would have just started to ignore a person like that as being completely irrelevant and unreliable. They would just stop listening to them and certainly would not repeat what they said on the news. They are totally Irrelevant!

When you have a close relationship with someone, a position of trust, if you tell that first lie, even a little white lie told to protect the feelings of that trusted friend, you will have totally destroyed that feeling of trust; probably will be gone forever! Tell me about it! Has that ever happened to you? We know! So, TRUST is the most important casualty of telling LIES!

Ah, but he was the President of the United States! Was he lying all the time because that was just his quirk of nature? I think not! When you are the President of the United States you are in a position of traditionally great respect by the entire world. Everyone, by nature, assumes that a leader of that standing would be telling the truth or they would not have that position. So, perhaps the lying was designed to destroy all TRUST! So, even before he became President, apparently, he was deliberately telling LIES to destroy everyone's trust in

46   our form of Government, the Rule of Law as well as the Constitution.

Then, he started making life difficult for the existence of NATO. He made demands upon each NATO nation to start "paying their fair share of the costs". In general, he seemed to do everything that he could to diminish the importance of NATO as well as to belittle them whenever he could. Apparently, he wanted to destroy the effectiveness of NATO - perhaps to help out his buddy from Russia. One must ask, who else?

Then, he started making statements to diminish the perceived stature of our military officers as well as the troops. Next, he took actions to disparage the image of our foreign diplomatic forces. Then, he moved on to the CIA and the FBI.

When it came to the respect for the principle of the three equal branches of government, he clearly chose to either not respect those precepts or to totally disregard that working relationship entirely. He refused to appear for subpoenas or hearings which shows a total disrespect for their place in the government or of their long-standing stature. In every instance, where it was possible, he showed a disdain for every form of tradition, institution or principle of this working government.

While President, he altered the way that the Justice Department worked by first appointing a subservient strongman into the office of the Attorney General. He probably asked him to swear an oath of allegiance to him instead of to the Constitution of the United States. He considered the AG to be his personal protector. In that role, his servant was asked to essentially weaponize the Department against his real and perceived enemies. That included those that he feared would be running against him in the next election. Perhaps, on his behalf, this was also done by the IRS. None of this behavior is conducive to a live, functioning Democracy. He was clearly already operating as a dictator in the role of President. Had any of this been known before now, there would have surely been an outcry from at least half of the US population!

There is a very important element of the extent we had gone towards becoming a Fascist Authoritarian Dictatorship (FAD) revealed by that last sentence. He had already required a very large part of the GOP to declare loyalty oaths to him; as demonstrated by the silence from every one of them when really disturbing things were revealed that he had done that were considerably outside of the bounds of Democratic behaviors! Believe me, they were frequent and many. A very large number weren't even known until after the January 6th Committee hearings. Even the most flagrant, like 1/6/21 that was seen by the entire world, was altered by the subservient MAGA GOP members as being nothing more than a peaceful Wednesday afternoon tour of Congress. What deceitful LIES!

As we look back over those past four years in office, it seems that everything that most people had assumed to be just a quirk of his personality, was likely a part of a long thought-out plan to totally degrade all trust in every part of this formerly working Democracy. The amazing part is that he was able to Normalize the destruction of so many important Democratic institutions, traditions and procedures in only four years of time. There had to be a master plan from another place that he followed. The biggest and the most important of the destructive maneuvers to destroy every trust in the most essential part of a Democracy was to propagate the BIG LIE about our elections. That destroyed the basis of Democracy!

Tyranny of the Few – The Absolute Tyranny of One!

We've finally come to the place where the totalitarian results of tyranny become extremely dangerous. That is when the rules of government (for example, within the Congress) allow a majority of a few or just one to make monumental differences in the outcomes and directions for our government and society itself. A majority of one completely changes a society from one direction to an entirely opposite direction, as if we were in a serious car crash. Stop to think about this for a moment. This is absolutely destructively monstrous. In earlier times this wasn't an issue because people then tended to be of the same general frame of mind. If they had differences of opinion about what it was they wanted to do, they were at least in general agreement that something good needed to happen. With common goals (even with differences of opinion on how to achieve those goals) they would at least work together toward those goals. To achieve this, they would compromise with conflicting factions. That's not happening now with the Freedom Caucus Terrorists.

Remember those definitions from <u>Sudden Theory</u>? <u>Sudden Theory</u> states that when you cross a single line in time or condition, in that microsecond everything transitions from one condition to another. It all changes dramatically like turning a light switch on in a pitch dark room. It is like Black and White, Night and Day, Life and Death, functional or totally inoperative. You see, the House and Senate are set up so that whichever party has a majority of one, it controls everything: committee assignments, who heads up each committee, which party sets the rules for the body of operation at Large and who controls which bills may be introduced to the floor for debate and eventually whether they will ever be voted upon. That microsecond transition is called a singular point.

In math, that would be called a "step function". On one
side your life is great and everyone is happy; on the other side you are dead and everyone is sad and mourning. That is how dramatic a "step function" in reality can be.

That is a far cry from transitions that change proportionally to how much of one faction is mixed with the other faction, like two metals in an alloy such as solder. So, 48% tin to 52% lead is only proportionately different from 52% tin to 48% lead, even though the situation has changed from a majority of lead to a majority of tin. That would be like being on a single negatively sloped straight line from (0, 100) to (100, 0). (% tin, % lead). The properties of the alloy of solder changes as those amounts change but they are not suddenly momentous or catastrophic, such as in a step functional change.

So, wouldn't a government be more democratic if it changed more like a metallic alloy than like ice going from a solid to a liquid at 32 degrees Fahrenheit under standard atmospheric pressure? If everyone in Congress came to that office with the understanding that they were working for the betterment of the country and fervently adhered to the letter of their oath (to defend the Constitution and the Rule of Law) the system would have (and has generally) worked for better than 240 years. But when you put even a small fraction of Anarchists, Nihilists or downright terrorists into that step function, it breaks down with very horrible consequences. The reason? Because with a step function system a very small majority completely changes the rules, the intent and the direction from one defending Democracy to one directed to the total destruction of the government and the Democratic way of life. One terrible outcome would be a FAD (Fascist Autocratic Dictatorship). In a government with the size and complexity as the US it is obvious that there must be hundreds of other parts whose outcome can be controlled by just one or two people!

50   The nine-member SCOTUS comes to mind. So, a 5:4 court can be diametrically different from a 4:5 court, even if that is just the difference of one person. We have just lived through such a situation with SCOTUS. The court has been generally dominated by more liberally centered judges or evenly split with perhaps one independent thinking justice that acts like a moderating swing vote. In some cases, that SCOTUS has sided with the moderates, and in others they have sided with the conservatives. When Supreme Court justices were approved with a strong consideration for being more centrist and being determined to try to adjudicate cases according to the law and the Constitution, even a difference of one vote could generally be tolerated. After all, the role of the Supreme Court is not to make laws but only to interpret them - or at least that was supposed to be the way that court worked.

When the Senate was stacked with an operational majority of conservatives, it eagerly approved radically biased justices that set up a totally biased court. This court was able to "legislate" from the bench and to essentially "pass" radical laws. Such a court, installed under Trump, "legislated" radical laws from the bench that go completely counter to common sense and 80% of the public interests. The outcome was the total reversal of Roe v. Wade that had been the Stare Decisis law of the land for 50 years. See how dangerously easily this was accomplished with very small majorities in just three parts of the government. With a radical president, a slight majority in the Senate, and a slight majority in the Supreme court: "Slam Bam, thank you Ma'am!" you have the basis for taking a democracy to a Fascist Autocratic Dictatorship (FAD).

The worst part: it is far harder to reverse this Democracy destroying Coup than it was to create it. Why? Because the Justices are appointed for life! Once in (and the new ones are young), they will be there for a very long time - unless they happen to die at a much earlier age than normal. Who knows?

There's an example of how important just one supreme court 51 seat in Wisconsin is tomorrow. That seat in tomorrow's election determines if elections will be gerrymandered to favor the MAGA GOP, how the State will rule on abortion laws and affects the outcome of national elections for decades. What about the other courts under SCOTUS? There are thirteen appellate courts under the Supreme Court in thirteen districts in the United States. These courts have many judges appointed by a radical Resident that were approved by a MAGA GOP majority in the Senate. They will affect us for a very long time!

Once there, these judges could be "shopped" to rule on elements of our normal lives with far-reaching, disastrous consequences. Such a judge might make a very biased ruling on the validity of birth control pills that have been used by women for over 20 years. One ruling by this one judge can effectively stop the use of this very effective drug forever throughout the entire United States. That isn't anything like how a democracy is supposed to work. That's one person making laws that apply to everyone. That is not a plurality of many but instead a dictatorship of one or two people. Normally, judge shopping is an abuse of process and is not permitted. There seem to be few practical options to prevent it from happening, or correct it once it has been done.

Putin's Puppet has totally corrupted the operational sanctity of critical institutions that not only allowed democracy to work but are actually very essential to it being able to work. There is no way that this puppet thought of these divisive techniques on his own. These are very sophisticated plans that can only be derived by a think tank committed to the total destruction of the democracy of the United States. There is one place where that has not only been a long-term desire but a fervent goal for at least a decade: Putin's Russia. Since the Miss Universe

52   pageant in Russia in 2013 there have been hundreds of documented direct connections between high-level Russian operatives and the former radicalized Resident. Why the Justice Department hasn't taken action to stop this menace before now is a puzzle.

There are so many more examples of how this Democracy becomes eroded while America worries about three or four balloons in the sky. Here's one to consider: Just a few people, armed with nothing more than a phone, are able to intimidate ordinary citizens that just happen to have very important jobs when it comes to the preservation of our democracy. They call and harass election workers with death threats to them and against members of their families. These people are a very low-cost, low-maintenance threat to the future of our democracy. If these calls end up causing these normally very effective and dedicated voting board workers to quit, those positions will immediately be filled with election deniers and MAGA sympathizers. Simply stated - with those MAGA agents on board, those election locations and election outcomes are not secure, nor can they be trusted. Mission accomplished with only one or two MAGA activists with nothing more than "burner" cell phones. It doesn't even require a gun or an AR-15. And how do you stop these one or two people from doing these deeds? Hey, they use "throw away" phones and only use them a few times. That makes it very hard to track because those numbers are not registered to a person's name or location. It is like a clean "Hit and Run".

Here is another example of how this minimalist erosion works to destroy the foundations of democracy. The Florida Governor adds a couple of very conservative board members to the board of a very liberal college in Florida. One of them is appointed as the new chairman of that board. Immediately, that chairman fires the former college president and suspends the contracts of all of the professors, including all tenured professors. He declares that all liberal inclusive diversity programs will be eliminated. He then bans the use of any College Board AP diversity programs or assistance on campus. Guess how that all will turn out! It is remarkable!

We are seeing so much more of this form of Tyrannical Intimidation with regard to school boards and city councils. Not only are there people who attend these board or council meetings and generally harass board members, but also go to raise totally bogus issues and circumstances in order to completely disrupt the normal flow of the meeting. This often results in either aborting or delaying the legitimate agenda for the meeting. If the harassment persists over a long period of time, honorable members become not only frustrated but annoyed to the point of quitting the endeavor entirely. They are then replaced by MAGA agenda advocates. There used to be a saying during the time of gold currency. When the gold became more valuable than the face value of the coin, it would be melted down and sold and thus gradually disappear. Gresham's law states that "bad money drives out the good".

You see, unfortunately, we are seeing this everywhere in our businesses as well as our government. It becomes the most sinister and dastardly method of subverting the effectiveness of anything of value. When there is a very effective employee that is dedicated to the goals of the enterprise and is fearless in its pursuit but is getting in the way of the grifting or corruption of a manager that manager just might feel threatened and might find a way of making that employee's work life a living hell until that employee gives up and quits. He or she is immediately replaced with a buddy or a kindred spirit crony that will keep his/her mouth shut. Worse yet, they may also be in on the con or the scam or have the same general views on the way things should be run.

54   This is also true in parts of the government like the House or the Senate of the United States. Right now the House has about 20 "bad seed" representatives whose purpose is to harass well-meaning and generally effective members of the house. This Tyrannical small group of a few members has but one purpose: to be totally disruptive of government. They're propaganda machines that are used to obfuscate the purpose of the government and to do whatever it takes to destroy it. By being the few that allow just one person at the top to prevent the approval of payment of America's debts that have already occurred - they can destroy the faith and credit of the United States causing a worldwide panic and a collapse of the world economy. If that happens, they have accomplished their goal and handed a major victory to Putin of Russia. Under most circumstances that would allow them to be characterized as World Terrorists - and Traitors to the United States of America. But now they are just considered as being legitimate representatives of the people of the United States. But one says; "Elections will take care of bad politicians." BS to that!

History should have taught us a lesson that the Germans didn't learn under Hitler. These seemingly small situations needed to be dealt with decidedly when they happened. And please no Kumbaya, or normal lengthy court deliberations or processes. No DOJ sitting around on its proverbial ASS for two years before even thinking about it. No, to save a democracy from this creeping Fascist Autocratic Dictatorship cancer, swift action must be taken immediately, much as you would disarm an active shooter in a grade school, University, bank, or rock concert. Saving a democracy under conditions that are set up by this kind of Terrorism may require a form of martial law and its procedures. Every minute of every day that these criminals are not in jail are days that they are planning, arming, recruiting, proselytizing and metastasizing. Germany found out far too late to be able to do much about it. What about the French and Polish resistance movements that actively worked in the '40s? Did you know that there was 55 also a "White Rose" German resistance during those early years to try to stop the transition to Nazism? Sometimes the court is way too slow to convict Terrorists in time to save us!

Even with the abundant successes that the Biden administration has had to reverse the atrocities of the prior administration, I feel it will neither be enough or soon enough to reverse the accumulated integration of Fascism that continues to propagate into small communities and in states like Texas and Florida. Inaction allows the terrorists a choice of places to plan and a luxury of time to recruit and implement future atrocities against the democracy of the United States. Allowing these MAGA Insurrection sympathizing people to remain in congress despite having broken their oaths of office is one of the dumbest things imaginable. Had the Democrats spent even one-day gaming out this conflagration and its possible outcomes, they might have had not only a plan but a commitment to take very deliberate and immediate decisive actions against the roots of this Fascist cancer that is growing very rapidly in our country. There are so many opportunities that were either missed or just plain ignored.

For example, those 84 or so MAGA "patriots" that signed their names to seven states' fraudulent electoral college documents and MAILED them to the National Archives - all committed mail fraud. The Postal Inspector force should have immediately arrested every one of those 84 signers of those fraudulent documents. This would have been a slam dunk because every one of them signed those documents that were mailed to the archives. This should have been done in no more than a day after its discovery to send a very stern and clear message.

All of those Insurrectionists that were in the capitol on 1/6/21 should have had plastic handcuffs applied, loaded into those many buses and taken to be housed in empty warehouses 56 until they could face trial. None of them should have been allowed to leave the premises. Every high-level person suspected of being involved should have had his cell phones, laptops, emails and files confiscated immediately. They should've been put on notice of their possible involvements.

Ninety percent of Americans have enjoyed the abundant freedoms and opportunities of living here most of their lives. Though they may generally appreciate that life, they seem to take it for granted and just accept it as the way it is and that it will be that way forever. As a result, they aren't passionate about having a need to defend it, like the Ukrainians feel about defending their homeland from Putin's war! On the nether side (in Hell), where the MAGA Terrorists have planned every hour of every day since at least 2013 (an entire decade) to destroy this very Democracy and life of America; they are hard core! They are fully radicalized opponents and activists dedicated to the total destruction of America. It is time to finally realize that they are not any of the Republicans that used to sit on the other side of the houses of Congress. Those days have been over for at least five years. We can no longer think of them as just being one of us with only a few differences of opinion.

Thus, not only do they have a very distinct advantage of total passion (like the Ukrainians) they act as if they have pledged a blood-allegiance and have sworn to do whatever it takes, however long it takes, despite how bad it gets, to execute their agenda to its horrible conclusion. That is total commitment! As a result, you cannot shame them, embarrass them, guilt them, humiliate them or even try to negotiate with them, because they will not be shaken from their oath or their cause.

By contrast, the Democratic majority clearly has been totally unaware that the other side is absurdly different than when they worked with them six years ago. They still think that the MAGA GOP would strive to be even more appealing to the electorate after failing so miserably in the '22 midterms. But 57 instead, they seem to double down on total insanity as if they already know that future elections will have absolutely no effect upon winning most of those seats. The 2023 news media is just now beginning to get the picture that they are so radical that they cannot be reasoned with in any way, shape, or form. The result is that radicalized terrorists are running circles around the Democrats by not doing anything that anyone would have expected them to do in the past. If what makes sense to normal people is white, they will always do black!

The result of the reasonably thinking non-passionate citizens, is that the terror group has been allowed to do absolutely crazy and totally irresponsible things. The worst part is that we and the media have wasted considerable, crucial time trying to figure out why anyone in their right mind would do any of these. Instead, had we all known three or four years ago that these were Fascist Terrorists instead of the slightly quirky pretending new Republican party we would have gamed out the dire consequences of their agendas. We would've planned out swift and effective measures at least three years ago to nip this (FAD) Fascist Authoritarian Dictatorship action in the bud. Pelosi should have kicked 140 GOP members out of the House for breaking their oaths of office and for their involvement in a 1/6/21 insurrection that nearly overthrew the government.

It is way past time to deal with these terrorists in a way to separate them from any contact with power or authority! Swift removal from offices in Congress and other positions of power would be a start. However, there is really only one thing that terrorists fully understand and that is a swift and lengthy incarceration in maximum term prisons. I just heard Ted Cruz grill AG Merrick Garland about keeping those people in Guantanamo retained for the rest of their lives. Isn't it interesting that he is talking about "eastern combatants" arrested in Iran in an unjust war that we started in order to 58 gain access to Iranian oil. The real danger is that we should be much more concerned about an armed medieval mob sent by the ex-president and his GOP party minions to overthrow the democratic government of the United States.

Putin and Trump are completely interchangeable with each other in many ways. They have the same goals, narcissistic psyche, desires, passions and, by far the worst of all: a mantra to never give up, apologize or admit failure or defeat. Like a cornered shrew, they will fight to the death before admitting defeat. That one thing makes them extremely dangerous because they will double down and double down till they, as a last resort, are tempted to do ostensibly absolutely heinous and destructive things. As a result of this new species in our midst, completely new measures and procedures might be considered in order to stop these dire cancerous nightmares! The very last thing that a robust democratic society needs is a cancerous threat from known domestic terrorists that are planning to kill thousands of law-abiding citizens in order to achieve their goals. This brutal intimidation by armed terrorists is one of their means of taking over our democracy. How different is that from a person with an AR-15 shooting and killing 20 children in a grade school? That threat must be eliminated.

I seem to remember the essence of names of movements in past situations that seemed somewhat effective in helping to keep societies free from the onslaught of terrorists like these. They had codenames like Swift-Arrow, Pitot Tube, Curare, Cross-Bow, Morning-Star, Black-Jack or Sling-Shot. They are sinister sounding but apparently they may have been very effective in doing what had been intended. Heaven help all of us if the terrorists have degraded our civilization that far. Just looking at what is preceding this trial in NY leads very sensible people to be afraid that this Nation may already be at that breaking point! There is just so terribly much to be lost!

A Run-on De Sand is Treacherous! 59

There is so very much wrong with the State that houses the so-called "woke " kingdom. Disney is celebrating its 100th year while that State is celebrating its 178th year. Both have had very long histories, but only one of them has been a beacon of wholesome family life and entertainment for its entire history. There can be nothing more motherhood, apple pie or American flag, for children, parents and their grandparents than Disney's characters, stories and immensely enjoyable theme parks. If what Disney represents is "woke", then 99% of American lives have not only been greatly enhanced by the "so-called wokeness" but "wokeness" has totally enriched them for their entire lives. Anyone who would try to destroy the beloved image of Disney could be totally insane (always a possibility), is desperately trying to be a FASCIST AUTHORITARIAN DICTATOR, or already is one. To mess with Disney would be even worse than the 3rd rail of politics.

As bad as that is, it is only the tip of a very cold iceberg! The list of totally Hitler-style FASCIST laws that have been passed in the last year is so long and insidious that there can be only one conclusion drawn: The State is already totally a FASCIST AUTHORITARIAN DICTATORSHIP (FAD). Let's just see how much REAL WOKENESS has been done to that State through enactment of very detrimental MAGA laws that adversely destroy the decades-known freedoms and fun-filled lives of the residents and visitors of states. These "woke" laws have been passed by a super majority of MAGA Terrorist radicals that are like sharks; having smelled the first hint of blood in the water they are having a feeding frenzy that they are not able to stop! The more they pass, the more they are driven to pass even more detrimental Fascist MAGA laws. They are so persistent in the destruction of peoples' lives that they must know (by some means not known to the rest of us) that neither elections, public opinions nor demonstrations will change 60   any of the results of their "shark frenzy." When society gets to that point, look out! You are very much in a Hitler's German FASCIST AUTOCRATIC DICTATORSHIP "venue" maze with no way out. It is essentially a done deal - caput!

Let's look at the horrific numbers! There's at least one new law that essentially eliminates abortion in the state. At least one that allows businesses to sue communities if they deem new regulations adversely affect those businesses. There are at least two that limit what state agencies can do to regulate the production of greenhouse emissions, the use of energy-saving materials in construction, or clean water. There is at least one that severely limits the availability of "Drag Queen" shows. There are at least two new laws that loosen up gun-carry and gun-safety Regs that had existed before - thus making it easier for more people to acquire and carry guns without restrictions. There are at least two that allow junk fees and eliminate rent stabilization that adversely affects hotel and hospitality regulations. There are at least two that adversely affect the rights of immigrants and their ability to work in the state. There are at least five that are completely averse to LGBTQ citizens and are especially cruel to their children! There is at least one to eliminate the Democratic Party in the state.

There are at least four laws that change who can select school boards, control the means to defund public education, control curricula and sex education and eliminate the use of "pronouns". Worst of all, they are taking over the boards of colleges, firing all of the faculty and president, banning all diversity programs and training, AP resources, black history curriculum, and replacing the president and faculty with right-wing ideologues to make these schools essentially totally useless as centers of higher learning and innovation. Seriously, it destroys any accreditation that matters to a student trying to get a great job or apply to a school for advanced degrees. All of these laws and actions essentially eliminate the residents of the state from ever obtaining a meaningful education or being able to get a real job - which essentially ruins their lives forever. There is also at least one law that supports union busting of public employee unions.

Finally, there are at least five laws that are designed to greatly restrict freedom of speech - one of the tenets of the constitution. There is the banning of books in schools and public libraries. There is a requirement for bloggers to register with the state if they are going to criticize the government or any part of it (for instance, politicians or the governor) or they might face serious fines. That one is a direct throwback to laws recently written in Russia and Hungary. There is a law to just not say "gay". There are laws that can apply a $35,000 penalty if you call someone a racist. And there is a law to prevent someone filming cops any closer than 30 ft. to the action.

The First Amendment provides that Congress can make no law respecting an establishment of religion or prohibiting its free exercise. It protects freedom of speech, the press, assembly, and the right to petition the government for a redress of grievances. The 14th amendment extends the prohibition to the states as well. Therefore, restricting speech or expression of words or values in books, movies, plays, dance or the arts is strictly forbidden by the government - even in the states, cities and towns. Freedom of speech and protests are the law of the land and are not to be breached by any government entity, period! Not even State governments!

Face it, when a government (city, state, or nation) passes laws that dictate severe fines, times in prison, or death to anyone for either doing something or not doing something; it is a Hitler, Mussolini, Putin, Orban, Kim Jung-un kind of law and has nothing to do with democracy and certainly is not for anyone's freedom, good life, happiness or pleasure! This kind 62 of law is not good for anyone. Period. Count on it! It is a very simple test that everyone can understand. It is a Fascist Authoritarian Dictatorship law! In addition to all of the obvious reasons why it is bad for many is the fact that even if it only affects a certain few; given enough time, it and its ilk will take on a form that at eventually will affect EVERYONE - even those who were so ill-advised as to promote it originally. It just is not suitable anywhere near a functioning democracy.

There appears to be so much more that is wrong with this State and its Governor. How is it that a governor in a state that just recently suffered hurricane Ian that destroyed a dozen towns and cost over $113 billion and 160 lives, is still popular? This is a governor that not only detrimentally attacked the "icon of wholesomeness" but has passed the largest cadre of freedom- destroying laws imaginable. How does he win elections in 2022 going counter to elections throughout the rest of the United States where politicians of his ilk lost so miserably? What is it about his election that goes so counter to the national trends? Is it possible that the elections controlled by his State are not up to the norms of more democratically controlled states? Is it possible that politicians in his state have no fear of the result of votes from their citizens? What is it that they seem to know about the integrity of elections that are not known by the voting public?

As a possible explanation to this apparent dilemma is a new police force set up by the Governor that deals exclusively with election crimes and voter fraud under the office of voter crimes and security housed within the Department of State.

These units, along with a fraudsters tip line, are used to intimidate voters and arrest those who they feel have voted illegally. Voter fraud in this State, as well as nationally, is almost non-existent. However, just the existence of this force can intimidate many normally voting citizens. Thus it has a horrendous effect!

This Governor has proposed to set up a paramilitary State Guard that works in parallel with the National Guard that he, rather than the federal government, would control. The Governor said this force of 200 would "not be encumbered by the federal government". A former Governor has stated that "no governor should have his own hand-picked secret police." This would be a police force that reports directly to the Governor, much as the "Brown Shirts" or the Gestapo did in Germany. How would that turn out for citizens or reporters that write something that goes against his desires or inclinations? Have you ever heard of anything that smacks of a Fascist Authoritative Dictatorship more than this? It certainly sounds like something that could exist in North Korea, Russia or Saudi Arabia. America is far better than this. How close is America to totally losing all of its freedoms? Not very far!

How can you compare criminal politicians that voided covid-19 protections that allowed 100,000's of citizens to die, or that started a Treasonous Insurrection that potentially could have killed 200 - 300 Congressmen and a Vice President of the US with a gunman that's shooting 20 kids with a rifle? Isn't it time to take a second (sometimes written 2nd) to amend the situation where "safe" politicians are using the power of their office and their ability to amend the laws to protect themselves and to keep them free from prosecution; to eliminate the threat, much as law enforcement would deal with a mass killer with an AR-15 in a bank, social hall or a school? Is it not true, when a situation is so dire that it requires quick action to mitigate it immediately before permanent damage is done to the entire nation - does that not call for immediate action in the second that it takes to amend the endangering threat to Democracy? Perhaps a White Rose might be a suitable tribute and a thank you for those who are brave enough to rid America of these insidious cancers that threaten our democracy every day so that we are able to live and speak freely about fear of Tyranny!

CHAPTER 16
We Have to THINK LIKE PUTIN

This title encompasses two meanings and texts that support them. The first Is: We need to be thinking like we had always been living in Russia and accustomed and aligned with life in that oppressive and authoritarian environment. The second is: We need to think like Putin in Russia. We need to know his playbook to understand the events that we are experiencing.

The first is an attempt to understand what is actually going on whenever the Resident seems to take some unexplained action. Such is the case when news people and we do not understand it or don't quite get it. "Why did he do that? What is going on here?" The reason for our confusion is that we have been living in America for all of our lives and we've lived under the Rule of Law and under the Constitution. We've lived a way of life that is of those tenets - not like living in Russia.

We tend to trust those in authority and give them the benefit of the doubt. We have always believed that they may have our best interests at heart. We are now dealing with techniques, behaviors, practices, procedures, dramas and goals that are more akin to a life that we might have experienced if we had lived in Russia. That is, living during the Revolution, Post Revolution, then under Stalin and now under Putin. That to us, is a totally foreign way of thinking and a kind of existence that we just do not comprehend; much less can even imagine.

We have grown up pretty much trusting the news - at least the reputable news like the New York Times, the Washington Post and the main networks like ABC, CBS, NBC, etc. There was a time when some newspapers were suspected of being owned by people who tended to be allied with a political genre and thus slanted. But we've now come to a time for several decades when newspapers and other media, if legitimate, must of their own accord and by their own direction, verify their sources before presenting the news with confidence. They can't take a risk of just guessing and hoping it will somehow come true after their story airs. It is totally inexcusable and not acceptable in our society to do that. Truth's the root to all freedoms and a vibrant Democracy.

We therefore tend to think that politicians, though possibly self-serving, are basically there to do the job that they were sent to do - to represent us and our interests. After all, this is America, a government *by* and *for* the *people*. It is not meant to be a government by and for corporations or the rich. Even though it's getting to be more and more like that, I digress. We tend to take it pretty much for granted. We tend to believe what has been said and we generally don't have to check it out since the newspapers and media make a determined effort to be quite accurate.

So when we hear or see something this Resident does that just doesn't seem to agree with our values, way of life, our beliefs or things that we think America stands for, we just don't understand. Because of our backgrounds, we tend to give the benefit of the doubt. We may assume that we must have mis-understood or perhaps we just didn't hear it right or correctly. Maybe we didn't get all of the facts. We tend to think; "Why would he do that?" It seems illogical that he's doing something that goes totally counter to common sense.

When he attacks gold star families relentlessly, for example, we think the man has absolutely lost his mind and has no sense of right and wrong. Has he no soul? Was he raised in a closet and fed through the door? No one does that. No One!

66 "Who would do that? Why would anyone do that? What is the point? That is just not done!" It is just not right and yet we've been assaulted by these very same things over and over again on a daily basis. Sometimes being assaulted a couple of times a day, as a result, it has become all too normalized. Yet, it is still foreign to our ways of thinking and living. Therefore, it cannot be resolved in our minds or souls. Pundits constantly wonder why he would do anything like that. Who on Earth would do that? Why would any sane man do that? Why would anybody do something so hurtful, harmful and just downright demeaning?

Our lack of understanding is perhaps because we haven't been living in a country like Russia. They lived under the Czars, then a Communist Regime and now under a "quote-unquote" Democratic Government. We don't instinctively understand what goes on in that kind of a world or society where it seems it's dog eat dog and every man out for himself with absolutely no trust of the government or of the politicians.

If we were to begin thinking as if we lived there, I think almost everything we have seen that seems so totally irresponsible, unlikable, unreasonable and unthinking would perhaps be better understood if: that's just the way life is. That's the way it's always been here in Russia and it cannot be changed.

So what is it we need in order to be able to counter what is going on? We all need to understand that form of life. We all need to understand their kind of thinking and what the consequences are. We need to be thinking as Putin thinks and what is in his playbook for America. In fact, I often say, when you hear the news and it's something that just does not seem to make any sense at all: just stop and put in front or behind the sentence; "in Putin's playbook". It may not be what we would like to hear but when you put it that way it all seems to make "sense".

So much "sense" it seems abundantly clear: It's to Russia's advantage and to America's disadvantage. It makes Russia more powerful, more significant on the world stage and for America to become a Second or Third World country by contrast. America would lose its power, lose its influence, lose its Integrity, lose its position in the world economically and politically. It basically becomes a destruction of what we know and what the world has known of the United States for centuries - seemingly a destruction of our way of life, future and our democracy. Putin must be laughing his ass off now.

We have to realize that this has been a dream of Putin and Russia for a very, very long time, particularly, after the demise of Russia as a great nation. As a disgraceful time for Russia, it's certainly not one for which to be proud. Putin is trying to change that radically and he's apparently found himself a meme that is very useful for him to tilt the playing field from down toward America to down toward Russia.

If there is a playbook, it likely has been generated in Russia, by think tanks that have looked at our constitution, our laws: the wording of it, the exercising of it and the way it is used. They have studied the laws, the procedures and traditions that have been accepted by almost everybody that runs for office. What they may have found is that the Constitution in general contains things like rules and laws but seemingly does not prescribe any real means to enforce them. Apparently, nothing is spelled out with any enforcement teeth.

68   For example, the emoluments clause. The Resident is not supposed to accept gifts or anything of value from other countries. That is the law. Dirt on an opponent in an election is something of value and the Resident is not allowed to ask for or to receive it. That would be breaking the law. Using his job to gain huge amounts of wealth from foreign governments is also breaking the law. This might occur when people come here representing foreign governments and rent rooms at his hotels or at his resorts. This might very well be considered as breaking the law of the emoluments clause.

So, what is the remedy? There seems to be no remedy spelled out in the Constitution and it appears that there is no legal entity that has standing in the courts to enforce that law.

In the past, whoever was in office simply respected the law as being what was expected of them. Tradition was being upheld and passed on from generation to generation. They didn't have to be caught, they didn't have to be chastised, they didn't have to be reprimanded, because we lived with the Rule of Law which is part of living under the Constitution.

Making this government work is just part of the goal that people who run for governmental offices tend to aspire to. People who basically want to do something good for the government and for the people tend to follow the laws. So they pretty much respect and don't break these laws that are in the Constitution. But when you have a person who believes that HE is the law, he just goes ahead and breaks these laws. Who is going to stop you? There's nothing in the laws of the Constitution that can actually be used to stop you from doing it. So why not just let it become the normal operation for evermore? That could only lead to a Government of Anarchy!

When we tried to go after the use of a hotel as breaking the 69 emoluments clause, the court threw the case out because we had no standing in the court. Apparently, no one has any standing because it can't be shown that they have been aggrieved by the breaking of the emoluments clause. The reason that the Constitution does not spell out who is aggrieved by the law being broken is that it is All of us - every citizen. We apparently have no standing in court. Aggrieved?

Well, how in hell are we going to go to court to stop him from doing this? So now that law seems broken forever. These and similar things, Putin and his think tanks must have figured out a long time ago. Are they passing that knowledge on to the man in the White House in a way for him to be using it to Putin's advantage and benefit? Woo Wee, what a pile of BS!!

If true, doesn't it just Torque you up something fierce? We are first just totally outraged and then completely frustrated because we realize we have no remedy. Is there no remedy? Is there actually no way to indict him or send him to jail? So the last thing you might do is impeach but that's probably not one of those offenses that would rise to the level of impeachment.

So, what is the other half of this dilemma? Putin, and possibly Kim Jung-Un (both strongmen) might be feeding the man in the White House deadly tricks and procedures that could take over this Government and make it like a dictatorship. This man seems to admire and fawn over these people who have the strictest kind of power that he seems to think is just absolutely the cat's meow. He seemingly wants to be able to act like a strongman and act as if he IS the United States and Congress doesn't matter; the courts and the Supreme Court don't matter - nothing seemingly matters! How convenient?

70   He apparently thinks he "IS" the United States so if he says something - he speaks for the entire United States.

How do we know that all of this razzle dazzle of going to see Kim Jong-Un about his nuclear war materials actually had anything to do with that subject? I believe their discussions were private. There seemingly were no notes taken. What if he was asking Kim Jong-Un to give him some tips on how to control a nation - absolutely? Can you give me some tips on what things I should do and in what order to absolutely take over a government and people? How do I take a smoothly running democracy and turn it completely into a dictatorship? And now if Kim Jong-Un has done all of this for him, might he not think he's in love with Kim Jong-Un and now he gets very nice love letters from him? Hmmm. Perhaps very interesting.

Well, yes. What do you think he's getting? Do you think he is getting the goods on how to destroy America? Do you think that Putin might be on the same track with all of these sidebar conferences they have at the G7, etc.? I can't imagine they're talking about whether Putin should do this or shouldn't do that. Is it possible that they were talking about how much he's done for Putin and what he might be intending to do when Putin suggests the next step? Like possibly taking over the Department of Justice, the Supreme Court, district courts, the military, FBI, CIA or, even taking over the State Department?

We know he denigrated the press completely, making it totally suspect and unreliable in people's minds. Then he denigrated the very members of Congress themselves. Denigrated law enforcement and the chief of law-enforcement, the FBI and CIA. Denigrated all of them so that no one had a sense of trust and safety under them! That's when you have a nation that cannot function anymore because it doesn't trust any of the institutions that it had loved, lived with and trusted all of our lives. If we lose trust - we lose all faith in our lives!

This is the rest of the story. If you look at the history of who's taken over countries, it all starts with the courts, then the control of news media, the justice system and the entire Congress - or at least the majority that is needed so there is no hope of getting anything accomplished. This could possibly lead to a process taking place that could very likely destroy all democracy as we know it. Therefore, this is all very Dangerous!

When you look at yourself and America. Tell me what you see. Take a look at the Department of Justice - DOJ. It was seemingly not working for us. It seemed to be working for the former man in the White House as his own personal fixer. He stacked the Supreme Court and then through Moscow Mitch put some 190 high-level justices in courts all over the United States. He constantly denigrated the press and particularly those most effective with behind-the-scenes investigations; to break through the most secret niches and crannies to discover what dastardly things were happening in those dark places.

And then he talked about Law and Order - that he was a Law & Order Resident! What Law & Order meant to the man in the White House apparently had nothing to do with the Rule of Law. He seemingly had no respect for the Rule of Law but seemed to use the law and the courts to exact revenge upon his enemies list or to litigate against those who would oppose him. He seemed to believe in courts to do his dirty work to go after people, defend himself, shift the odds of the playing field so that he would win and all of the rest of us just might lose.

He loved the military and loved policemen and police people. Why? Perhaps he seemed to think of them as the enforcers of

72   his edicts. Even though he denied it - he seemed to be a "looking the other way kind of guy" tacit supporter of White Supremacists and seemed to allow them license and cover to do whatever they want even though he denied knowing any of them or having any interest in them at all. However, his actions certainly seemed to belie those claims as his actions almost always seemed to contradict everything else that he claimed.

We are so close to the end that it is scary. We seem to have half of the Congress basically doing Putin's dirty work for him. It appears they are taking his misinformation and selling it as being the real skinny. Putin must be laughing his ass off because when he puts something out it seems half of the Congress runs with it as if they're spreading cow pie manure.

Congress seemingly is now unwittingly working as Russian agents entirely against America's best interests. Oh God love-em, that just sucks horse-pucky! At this point we are at the end of a string that is close to breaking. We've tried impeachment. It was thwarted. Now we have one last shot and that's the election. Damn it. We've got to get it right. We have to get it right and keep it right and destroy this cancer that seems to be eating all of us and would affect all of our lives for a very long time if we fail. '"Never" has a very ominous ring to it.

* * * * By William Shakespeare: from Macbeth.   Tomorrow, and tomorrow, and tomorrow, Creeps in this petty pace from day to day, To the last syllable of recorded time; And all our yesterdays have lighted fools The way to dusty death. Out, out, brief candle! Life is but a walking shadow, a poor player, that struts and frets his hour upon the stage, and then is heard no more. It is a tale Told by an idiot, full of sound and fury, Signifying nothing. ...

How often must we reflect upon these sentiments lest we be heard from no more!! Our duty as citizens is very clear!

CHAPTER 17

Where Are the 12 DECENT PEOPLE?

I can't tell you how many times during those 4 years in the W H I cried out after a long news-day: 'where in hell are 12 decent, law-abiding, upstanding people who might march into the Oval Office, wrap that former Resident in a straitjacket, shove him into a closet and put a cardboard cutout of him behind the desk? So many times, it seemed - sometimes on a daily basis - for the things done to this country - seemingly not for it, that seemed so awful, so terrible, so demeaning and downgrading to the dignity of these United States - that somewhere, somehow, there had to be at least twelve, reasonable, honorable, clear thinking, decent, capable people that knew what's best and must take action to mitigate it.

For example, who in the hell in their right minds would let the Resident have a meeting with Putin by himself with not even note takers, or if there were notes, allow them to be destroyed? The very same thing goes for those meetings with Kim Jong-Un. What kind of Insanity would it take to even think that a meeting would be in the best interests of the United States Government, particularly if there were suspicions there may be close functional ties between Putin and the Resident that may have led to his selection in 2016? Even if these were only suspicions, no Board of Directors of a company would ever allow such an abortive meeting to occur. Where is the Board of Directors of the United States who could've stepped in and said to the Resident: "I'm sorry; that is not allowed by our Charter, our Mission Statement or our operating principles."

When he goes to see Kim Jung-un, presumably to talk about the Denuclearization of North Korea (because the meeting is private) might he in fact be talking about how to take over the freedoms of a Democracy? A Democracy such as the

United States? What steps to take first? What were the next steps? What steps to secure the results in an irreversible way that cannot be overturned except by a foreign army as the free world did in the 2nd world war?

We are seemingly like the people of Europe during World War II, who knew all too well what had happened to their life and their freedoms. They were well aware of the results of this kind of takeover but were totally helpless to do anything about it, to stop or change it or alter it in any way. It had gone past the Rubicon - the point of no return - forever. We are seemingly at that point now with only one last hope remaining. The hope of the 2024 election - which we know all too well - that Putin may have his thumb on the scales and might do his best to tilt the playing field so that no matter how many of us vote - the Resident may still be able to be re-elected.

If that happens, we might as well all become refugees and try to find some other place to go and live - perhaps Australia, New Zealand, Canada or Mexico. Any other place but here. The results would be too devastating, too complete, too horrifying to contemplate. We are already there in some aspects. So much so that I say: people, open your eyes and see what's already happened in just the last month and know that this has to be stopped, to be reversed. This cancer must be eliminated now. Hey, you GOP rallying tribes? You may be detrimentally affected even more than anyone else by the results. Your lives likely will be ruined even more than the rest of us. Thank you so GODDAMN MUCH for your just looking the other way!

While I'm on the subject, where are those 12 reasonable men in Congress or Governors who everyone knew at other times to be clear thinking, rational public servants that would've known what to do rather than be sycophant lackeys? DAMN it all!

1. A truth can form only a single line between points A and B.
2. There's only one line, of many, that's true between A and B.

In other words, if there are two or more lines between A and B only one can be true. So, if there are many lines between A and B - ALL OF THEM are LIES except possibly one, because only one of them can be the truth! Should be so very obvious.

Lies, however, can form thousands of lines between A and B. If many lies are generated between A and B, perhaps tens or thousands of them, it is a moot point because it is almost impossible to find one truth out of hundreds. Therefore, If you never tell the truth and everything is a different lie, then you are generating myriads of lies - that all just might appear to many people as being the truth. But, by an overwhelming history, perceptive ones know; *all of them must be considered as lies*.

This allows you to pick the best one later to answer a question. You can point to THE one lie that agrees with the challenge and therefore ignore the hundreds of others that don't. Guess what? By this M.O., you can always have the right answer for the situation at hand. By this process you cloud the issues and are obfuscating the truth in a way that it's almost impossible for anyone to distinguish what is true anymore. Almost impossible from now on! Remember, lies are the path that destroys Trust!

If we are drowning in a sea of Lies and reaching for the single truth, it is impossible to find it in that sea of Lies. Lies and Truth, by then, all look alike and seemingly every one of them could be the truth. But they're not!

76   So if the White House says something about alternate facts - and everyone knows that there are no alternate facts - it's likely intended to obfuscate away from the actual truth.

This is simple enough to understand but what does this really mean? I suppose it means at the very least that you can be everything to everyone and can easily satisfy everyone's needs at the moment - to their satisfaction. Everyone hears exactly what they want to hear and nothing contradictory. However, as bad as it sounds, it turns out to be far more sinister than that. It Is, orders of magnitude, far more sinister - branching out - possibly to be even more totally destructive.

When a democracy is swimming in a sea of lies and cannot find the truth, it is going to drown in that sea, leading to a total disaster. Democracy and the rule of law depend upon knowing the facts or the truth to make the right decisions or have convictions. Lawmakers cannot construct or pass laws if they don't have a true basis upon which to build them. They must have the truth - the facts - on which to make the right decisions. It is impossible to fashion laws or enact legislation if none of the basis has any truth in fact. All are considered as lies and so the source must always be *considered irrelevant*!

If it's based upon lies, democracy dies! A democracy cannot exist in a sea of Lies with no basis, no facts and no foundation whatsoever to build upon. If you are in the sea of lies, what difference does it make if you add just a few more drops of water (propaganda)? Drip by drip our democracy washes away in a total tsunami of lies and ceases to exist. We might as well just kiss it goodbye! Just think back on the past six years and what is it that you really recall the most? One thing that stood out in those four years is that the Resident in the White House had told more than 30,000 lies in roughly fourteen hundred days. That could be 21 Lies per day or several per sentence. Did any of them help any of you understand what was going on? Have any of those lies helped explain how he was selected rather than the one who won 3 million more popular votes? Have any of them confirmed what this person promised he would do to help you, the American People? Did any of those lies help exonerate this person or defend his behavior in the Ukraine, Russia or North Korea?

Many more pages with similar questions and you'd still not run out of examples of what this person seemingly did not do for you through lying! Think back. I think you could fill five more pages of such questions by yourselves. Fact number 1: it's generally believed he rarely told the truth. The Resident of the United States - the leader of the Free World -The Beacon of democracy MUST NOT TELL LIES. The very nature of this post - its position, its prestige, its insights, just couldn't be filled by a person that tells lies! It does not work for America or for the world. Truthfulness should've been the absolute minimum requirement to be allowed to occupy that high position.

How many wrongs make a right? How many lies make a truth? One? ten? How many lies did it take to make our one truth? 1,000, 10,000? It turns out, it took 30,000 Lies to make out one truth: that this man seemed unfit to be the Resident of the United States. Always telling the truth, should be the first absolute minimum requirement for the job of President of the United States. Always being truthful is the first requirement of any job application that I've filled out whether I've been successful or not. Why wasn't it the absolute first requirement to be qualified to be President of the United States - the most powerful position in the world? Was it just overlooked?

78   Did we miss it somehow? Was the box just not checked? Please explain to me how this could have happened!

How many lies did it take to *Fake* America great again? How many lies did it take for Mexico to pay for the wall? How many lies did it take to bring jobs back? How many lies did it take to try to show that jobs came back to the United States when it seemed that the net-net was nearly zero? How many lies did it take to Drain the swamp? How many lies did it take to get the farmers' soybean markets back into China? How many lies did it take to get North Korea to denuclearize its military? How many lies did it take to save the souls of those poor children and families at our Southern border?

How many lies did it take to keep the world from knowing how much Russia did in the 2016 election? How many lies were told about talks with high-level Russian contacts during the campaign? How many lies did it take to cover up those vital connections - Russia - seemingly in the campaign? How many lies were used to cover those possible connections with high-level Russians during the campaign? How many lies did it take to claim that Russia had nothing to do with the 2016 campaign? How many lies did it take to claim his inauguration had the largest crowd ever - particularly bigger than Obama's? How many lies did it take for Putin to know better than our own secret service and Intelligence and Security Agencies?

How many lies did it take to claim that the denuclearization treaty with Iran was terrible and needed to be abandoned? How many lies did it take to claim that the Paris global warming accords needed to be abandoned? How many lies did it take to claim that there is no such thing as global warming, whether man-made or not? How many lies did it take to claim that Saudi Arabia had nothing to do with the brutal Khashoggi assassination? How many lies did it take to claim that NAFTA was a terrible agreement and then replace it with

NAFTA2 essentially the same as NAFTA but with some benefits the Democrats added before it passed?

How many lies did it take for an attorney to claim that the Resident had absolute inalienable rights under Article II that - whatever he believes is justified - cannot be challenged? How many lies did it take to cover up a Ukraine Bribery and Extortion scheme? How many lies did it take to try to promote the Putin misinformation that Ukraine interfered in the 2016 election instead of Russia? When did we stop hearing possible lies about the independence of the DOJ from the Resident of the United States?

I could've gone on with this list but you knew them better than I did. You know them all! You've seen them - you've heard them - you've lived them. Where does it stop? When do we finally take this to heart and eliminate a cancer that has slowly grown into the very soul of America and is devouring our Democracy? How many more lies will it take? Another thousand, ten thousand? Will it, perhaps, take thirty thousand or more?

None of our lives have that much time left to survive this. Folks, here's the deal. We're no longer approaching the brink! We have already crossed the red line, the Rubicon. We have gone beyond the point of possibly no return by breaking, destroying and abandoning the Rule of Law - the very heart, soul and basis of this Democracy. When we totally ignore the tenets of the Constitution and the tenets of the Rule of Laws and principles; we no longer have this beloved Democracy that we have loved and shared for over 240 years. It just could cease to exist. FOREVER! We've got to defend Democracy!

CHAPTER 19
Rules, Procedures, Agreements, Laws, Treaties
This is a tough one and it requires a lot of analysis.

I was watching a NHL hockey game while waiting to have my hair cut. There were highlights from a particular game between two prominent Canadian teams. There was one team member in particular that started off "slashing" other players (seemingly, on a regular basis). These, then, usually resulted in some sort of immediate retaliation, such as a body slam or escalating to the gloves coming off and ending in a full-bodied fight. The frequency of this, and the fact that this particular player seemed less interested in the puck or actually playing the game, made me think that his role was almost entirely outside the norms or the rules of the game on purpose.

This became extremely clear when his aggressive actions escalated to far more dangerous moves such as intentional "boarding". At one point, he accelerated himself into slamming a "defenseless" goalie into the boards so hard that his helmet came off and his face hit the plastic shield so that he was knocked out, ending up in a pile on the ice. After that, other players piled onto him. The goalie was so bad off that he had to leave the ice. The thing that amazed me was that the referee only gave him a minor 2 min penalty. Expulsion seemed right.

So, here is the point. Even in a game such as Ice Hockey, there have to be rules that are agreed upon to make the game work. Obviously, these have been worked out over time with trial and error and as each new situation presents itself, so that not only will the game survive but that the players have a decent chance of surviving as well. They are not made up just to be contrary - there is a very definite purpose; making it fair!

So, there are rules of the game, not to just be arbitrary or contrary, but to allow the game to work and to be equally fair to both sides. This ensures that the games are not just interesting but the sport will not only survive but will thrive!

So, what was this one player doing in this game? He clearly was not "playing" the game. He also was clearly not abiding by the rules of the game. What was His game? He was practicing Asymmetric Warfare! By breaking every rule that everyone else was obliged to follow, he was taking exceptional advantage of all the other players in that game. To add insult to injury, he was "Getting away with it!". That, in itself, is a double slam in the realm of Asymmetric Warfare! There's way too much of that now!

By such extreme intimidation and by causing severe injuries to the opposing players, his team had extraordinary advantages over the other team that would surely result in an overwhelming win for his team. He was after "winning at all costs" and total control and power over all of the others. The fact that the Referees either wouldn't or couldn't do anything about it certainly assured a win for his team - even if they were inferior to the opponent. They were for power and control only - not to be playing a fair game. Now, you know that Ice Hockey is a rough sport and the crowds expect (no demand) to see a lot of "rough stuff" on the ice, but there are rules and norms that were clearly exceeded in this game and by this player!

Does anyone see a metaphor coming here? Games are something all of us can understand quite readily and enjoy because of the way they are played - with rules that work. Football, Basketball, Baseball, card games, board games, sidewalk games, even gambling games all have rules to be followed that allow them to work, so the players, as well as the observers, are able to enjoy them to the fullest. Sometimes

82   in football games a defensive player will "take out a player" in a way that looks legal, but may hit him so hard that he is out the rest of the game. Clearly, a player that plays outside the rules of a game is using a kind of Asymmetric Warfare.

There seems to be no way to sugarcoat this, so I just have to say it. The Resident, having been the chief executive of a corporation/LLC (whatever) seemed to act as if he worked in an entity that had no Board of Directors. I could be wrong about that. Apparently, his experience as the boss is that nobody was above him who can say; "I'm sorry, but you can't do that. That is not what is done. That's not in the best interest of this organization; you could go to jail" - as very well it may be against the law or for some other understandable reason.

No matter the reason or the circumstance, that is the way he seemed to believe that he can work as the Resident of these United States. Well, it just does not work that way in the United States (or at least it used to not work that way). The government is broken up into three equal parts that provide checks and balances on each other and over the entire system. All of them (without exception) work for us, the people of the United States - their employers. They all take an oath of office to protect and defend the Constitution and its tenets - including the rule of law, which is the very basis of democracy. To do otherwise is to destroy the very foundation and existence of this great nation.

What seemed to be observed is that he didn't believe in the rule of law as it may apply to him. Perhaps he thought he 'IS' the law, to the extent that whatever he said actually became law. No need for legislative or judicial branches. There's an ugly name for just this thing. You all know it - now say it to yourself out loud and hear how bad it sounds in your ears. Just say it!

Apparently, he didn't believe in the rule of law for himself but that didn't mean that he didn't believe in the use of law to be used against others. The courts seemed to be ineffective against his behavior, but he apparently loved using the courts to go after others in legal actions imposed upon them.

There's an interesting dichotomy - Law and Courts for others but of no value against him. Apparently, he thought he could ignore them as being irrelevant when it comes to himself. He loved to use the courts to keep people from getting things from him (all the way to the Supreme Court if necessary) but when the courts rule against him it tends to be ignored. I mean, what were they going to do about it? Who's going to make him obey the court order? Does that sound familiar again? I mean, does that not sound like that ugly word that we were saying out loud before? Probably! Yes! But ... I Hope Not!

Apparently, there was no Board of Directors that could say, "I'm sorry, in the Federal Government we don't do that and you can't do that." That Board of Directors normally would be a large group of people with enough clout to walk in and say "No, this just isn't going to happen. No, that's not the way it is." That group seemed to be the bulk of the GOP party that's in the government. Those that normally were rule of law - constitutional law-defending and abiding people, for whatever reason, were then looking the other way. Perhaps they felt that was alright: "He's our guy; he can do no wrong."

All we can say is, if that's the deal (and there seems plenty of feedback to indicate that's what is believed by his base), then this nation seems to be in a great deal of hurt and trouble and may have really hard times in the future. Perhaps worse than this horrible pandemic we will likely suffer much worse, serious consequences for a much longer time. God help us all!

84   The rule of law seemed to be under more severe attack shortly after the Mueller report. This attack seemed to be coming primarily from the one part of the government that was charged to defend the rule of law and to defend the people of the United States against internal and external threats. Instead, the DOJ seemed more interested in trying to eliminate the existence of the Mueller report and any or all charges against people that may have been charged as a result of the Mueller investigation.

Let's see if I can put this in perspective. A person who is not part of the government in any way calls a foreign diplomat of a country that has just been sanctioned by the United States government for election meddling. He implores them to not reprimand in kind but to wait until the new government is installed when things might be 'taken care of'. That violates a federal law - the Logan Act - enacted January 30, 1799. It criminalizes negotiation by unauthorized American citizens with foreign governments having a dispute with the United States. The intent behind the act is to prevent unauthorized negotiations from undermining the present government's position. Since this law was violated over an issue affecting the outcome of our most sacred institution - voting for the highest office in the land - it represents the greatest security and sovereignty threat that is possible to the United States!

Clearly, this is of the highest security interest that can be: the very basis of our democracy: involving both the rule of law and the complete integrity of our ability to elect officials and governments completely free of any foreign interference. After pleading guilty twice, the defendant changed his plea to not guilty and the DOJ decided to drop the charges as being of no consequence to national security. Ok, so, just how many criminals will suddenly want to do this just to get out of jail?

MIGHT as well set up VOTING BOOTHS in MOSCOW

Boy, we have really done it; haven't we? We have crossed the Rubicon. This impeachment inquiry really opened up a huge can of worms that were crawling beneath the surface - out of sight, until the Whistleblower brought them to the surface to be seen. What forms these worms have taken have expanded our imagination into almost anything, if not everything, that can possibly go wrong if a Resident were to have been chosen by a foreign country - bent on destroying the United States.

It seemed much of what was found during the impeachment investigation regarding possible bribery and extortion of Ukraine, using taxpayer money and the high position of the presidency, may have been specific to a type of extortion in order to aid and abet the Resident's chances in the 2020 election. However, to those of us who have suspected this from the beginning, it seemed to validate the notion that this is not a unique single first-of-its-kind incident. What has been shown is that this may have been an ongoing activity that might have gone on during the 2016 campaign as well.

Even though we knew Russia was highly involved in the voting manipulation of the 2016 election in favor of the Resident, we have had some doubt as to whether there was a cross connection between his campaign and Russia. The Ukraine investigation seemed to dispel any doubt that this has possibly been going on during the '16 campaign and perhaps as far back as the 2013 Miss Universe pageant in Moscow.

The Ukraine investigation seemed to reveal a very ugly image of what we might've imagined before - it may be only the tip of the iceberg. This possible involvement against the United States may have been going on at a much deeper, broader

86   level than anybody could possibly have imagined before. It seemed improbable he was elected based on what he did himself. This then begs the question. If he used international interference and cooperation to help get himself selected, we might just as well drop the middleman and set up voting booths in Moscow, Beijing, Riyadh and Pyongyang.

Hey, despite that it seems totally unreasonable, the facts seem to show we are pretty much matched nearly 50/50 - Democrat vs Republican - when it comes to elections. From the Democrats' standpoint it seems like it should be 90 Democrats, 10 Republicans, but for whatever strange reasons it doesn't turn out that way. Okay, if that's the case, why do we even bother setting up voting booths here in the United States since that notion will pretty much cancel itself out.

As a result, the election would be determined, as it might have been in 2016, by interference from a place like Russia. If that's the case and we're going to have it normalized, we might as well get used to it. We might as well just set up voting booths in Moscow, Beijing, Riyadh and Pyongyang and let them determine the outcome of our election for us - pretty much as they very well may have done in 2016.

Think how much easier that would be for people in the U.S. They don't have to worry about getting to the voting booths on days that they work. They don't have to get themselves registered. They don't have to make the effort and stand in those long lines. Think of the cost reduction if we don't have to have precinct voting committees in each state and we don't have to pay for voting machines or places to poll. Just have it all done from outside the country the way it has seemingly been done in the last major election of 2016. Hey, if the result is essentially going to come out the way, Russia, or Beijing

wants it to come out, then let them have at it. We just
become shadows of ourselves and, as the old saying goes, wash our hands of it and accept whatever the results may be.

I mean, what's the difference if we have crooked judges at the Super Bowl and we BET our retirements, homes, jobs, futures on the outcome of the Super Bowl? Hey, whatever happens when the crooked judges make their decision - that's what we have and that's what we will live by. How bad can that be?

Doesn't that just sound great to a casual, laid-back, perhaps lazy electorate? It sure saves a lot of stress on the brain listening to candidates bragging about their capabilities and listening to the harangue between them or the dastardly ads that they run against each other. What could be even more simple, what could be most easy, what could be more insane? Laissez-faire and C' est la Vie. Nobody gets upset. Cousins and uncles; fathers and daughters don't get into huge knock-down drag-out fights at Thanksgiving or Christmas. We just all agree to get along and let it all roll out like in Russia?

Tongue-in-cheek? Yes, tongue-in-cheek. Where in hell are those Republicans who used to believe in the Constitution, swear by the rule of law and the tenets of the Constitution and who hated Russians and called them 'Pinko Commie Lovers'? Where in hell are they when the country seems to be going to hell in a Putin basket? What do they think they are going to get from this "person", that it's worth scrapping everything to follow the Pied Piper? Where is the Lemming - Aid? Even though lemmings don't commit suicide jumping off the cliff as in the Myth we might as well believe that they do. So these people, who are following this "person", are basically running off the cliff - and don't seem to stop to see, care or even consider that the cliff is coming up just ahead.

88   They don't even think in terms of a cliff but instead they may think they're doing something spectacular, going up a hill and going to have wonderful times. Well, when it all hits the fan they are going to be part of what hits the fan. And you know how the saying goes; what hits the fan, the fan makes into mincemeat. Enough said! Poor Pinko Commie Lovers!

*Just a footnote: about Amoral vs. Immoral. These Concepts - throughout the writing of this book - seemed to keep popping into my head as to what really is the meaning and what is the difference as if there was such a deep-down significance for this book? I, seemingly, was compelled to find out. Perhaps the reader can extract some significance to the connection.

Both have to deal with right and wrong and therefore if you don't have the correct definition they might be confusing.

- Amoral; means having no sense of either right or wrong. Doing something and just not knowing better.

- Immoral; describes someone who does know the difference, doesn't care and does whatever he wants - possibly for his own benefit without concern for others.

Oh, why oh, why, for the life of me, why do these things keep popping into my head throughout the writing of this book? Do you, as a reader, get the significance? Can you tell me why these things are apparently significant in my mind as I was going through the process of the writing of this book? I bet that you can - without hesitation or contemplation.

These Defenders of the CONSTITUTION
The Dark Force Vs the Deep, Dark State

By the end of 1/31/20, the Senate was so goddamn awful that perhaps those Senators might see themselves in a video or just wake up and feel just how mean-spirited they were. Many, if not most, at one time, were normal, living, thinking, reasoning people. Perhaps they might wake up completely horrified and admit "how cruel, debased, and mean-spirited we all seemed. That is not who we were! That is not who we are! That is not what America is about! That's not how Americans got to where we were until two or three years ago. It is not how America must be now and in the future!"

So how did it come to this? The gate opened by the apparent disrespect for the Rule of Law, followed shortly thereafter by a road that could lead to the collapse of democracy of America and its venerated position in the world. This cannot be, must not be! This cannot stand even if it takes a hand from heaven reaching down to intervene.

We've heard many times before that power corrupts and absolute power corrupts absolutely. Seventy-seven percent of America is now asking what were you all thinking? To whom were you giving allegiance to do his bidding when you have committed to work for the people for whom you are bound by oath to serve? We are the citizens of the United States! Do you not remember us? "We The People?" We are your bosses - you cannot be influenced to blindly follow some Svengali!

It is unfathomable how you can live with yourselves, much less with your families and friends! Look in the mirror. Look at yourselves! How can you stand yourselves? How can you face your families, including your children, when they know better

90   than you what damage you may have done to the American Constitution of this wonderful place: a place in which they, by your inaction, someday, may be required to live in which may have nothing of value to live for!

NO One should have such power. Not anyone. No One must be above the law, not even the Resident of the United States. So many of us, (the majority of us) feel that you need to take a very hard look at yourselves and get a firm grip on what has always been right for America. Do your job - you took an oath to work for us and defend the United States. Now, just do it!

Oh, Moscow Mitch. You seem to stand up for Putin's ultimate destruction of America. You must be so very proud! You stood up there so proud like a peacock. You seemed to imply that you were in control; could do anything. You can do it all and will do it all and they just cannot stop you, no matter how totally valid their evidence is or is presented. Just let them try.

Whoever heard of any trial in America where the jury foreman runs the trial, much less coordinates trial strategy with the defendant? The jury foreman works for the court, not the person on trial! That's no trial. That's a sham trial! Well, as Goliath found out, 'Pride goes before the fall.' 'The bigger they are, the harder they fall.' May we soon all hope to take comfort in these Words.

GOP Senators: What can you possibly tell your 12-year-old son or daughter when they know you voted to not only ignore overly compelling evidence that might have saved this nation from possible national security risks but also condemned this nation to a path to a dictatorship. Do you know? Have you ever really stopped a moment - like in Church - to seriously think about it or taken it to heart?

Here is quite an intriguing thought! When you unleash
the glint of the brandishing sword, you are never quite sure
where it goes, where it is going to come back, where it will
land or what it might slay. You may actually be mounting your
heads on your own pikes by becoming the victims of this
apparent, senseless abdication of Justice: the diminishing of
America that has seemingly been unleashed. This may very
well come back to bite you all in the proverbial butt!

There must be an epitaph for this. I can't quite figure out what
it is. But, by God, we have come to such a terrible place in
such a short time, we must have hope that there is a way to
get better (and very soon) and do it completely.

 *Author's updated note: Things had so dramatically changed
in just those last 2 months, when the deadly onslaught of the
Covid-19 virus hit, that the Impeachment trial was almost
totally forgotten. It is unthinkable to suggest that Heaven had
sent it but, biblically speaking, is that not what is often implied
in the "Book" when pestilences are described or discussed?
For Example:

Deuteronomy 32:24
They shall be wasted with hunger, and devoured by plague
and poisonous pestilence; I will send the teeth of beasts
against them, with the venom of things that crawl in the dust.
or
Ezekiel 14:19
Or suppose I were to pour out my Fury by sending an
epidemic into the land, and the disease killed people and
animals alike.

CHAPTER 22
The Honor and REPUTATION of America

There was a time when people in the United States valued the reputation and honor of the US - both here at home and around the world. We were the beacon of Democracy and the fountain of generally honorable images and perceptions. Our word was trusted, as well as treaties that were considered binding. We could be trusted to not arbitrarily renege on a treaty or suddenly decide that now we don't think it's right and just cancel it unilaterally.

What we saw in the 45th President's years was the cancellation of the Paris Climate Accords, the JCPOA denuclearization agreement with Iran, NAFTA with Mexico and Canada and the Trans-Pacific trade agreement. That's just the tip of the iceberg. By derogatory rhetoric, our relationships with our allies around the world, and, in particular, NATO, were severely undermined. Our world image and prestige, as a result, were very much in jeopardy. Therefore, the world leaders tended to be looking to Russia and China for guidance and alliances.

So what did this mean? In just four short years, our Role (as the beacon to the world for Democracy and a world leader) seemed to have plummeted and been severely damaged; hopefully not irreversibly. Actions (as seen implemented nationally and worldwide) were, or are nearly, irreversible. Our Institutions that supported us so ably for years have been so completely diminished, under-staffed, underfunded and under-managed by appointees not approved by Congress that may have become mere skeletons of themselves. Traditions that have regulated us and have maintained this democracy have been ignored, set aside or just outright eliminated. Apparently, these very detrimental things have been totally normalized and makes it very hard to go back to what worked.

What do we do? Whatever do we do? With just 4 more years of this there absolutely would be no going back. In fact, the changes are now so rapid in a certain direction that in far less than 4 years this democracy would be so totally changed into something entirely different - something that may not be so pleasant or desirable. 300 million people would suddenly have to find someplace else to live and something else to do. There's no way that anyone who has lived here even 10 years would want to live under a new regime or direction like that.

Disturbing news was heard that the Justice Department had been trying to enact changes to citizens' right laws such as - Writ of Habeas Corpus - that fundamentally were to secure freedoms and our rights. This was seemingly done under the premise of enacting emergency laws justified by the Covid 19 virus pandemic. It seemed that there was a lot of that going around in Europe in the mid 40's - and in other countries which we now consider under less than desirable regimes.

Emergency laws are supposed to be laws that revert back when the emergency is over, but history has pretty much shown that once the law gets installed (depending upon the administration at the time) they may just forget to change it back and it could become a permanent part of the new way of life. These things tend to happen way too often, especially if a new authoritarian government has been formed.

Habeas Corpus is an important part of the Constitution. The Constitution specifically includes the Habeas clause in the Suspension Clause (Clause 2) located in Article One, Section 9. It states, "The privilege of the Writ of Habeas Corpus shall not be suspended, unless in cases of rebellion or invasion when the public safety may require it." Enough Said?!

CHAPTER 23
The ENEMIES LIST and the DARK STATE

Now we **turn to "enemies-lists". It's rumored that the Resident may have worked on them since before the impeachment proceedings started. From the beginning, he talked about the Deep Dark State. Those were the people who had been "purposely left behind" in key positions by the previous administration to prevent the new Resident or the party in power from accomplishing their goals.**

If you ever doubted that the Resident might have been tied to Putin by a tether or by the hip - you might well kiss that doubt away right now. By these two terms (Enemies Lists) it might be confirmed that this connection may go back at least to 2015. These two terms are directly from a dictator's playbook - possibly like Putin's Playbook. These terms are just never ever used in a democracy like the United States - not ever! They are an anathema to a well-functioning democracy and totally alien to its ability to remain as a democracy. They are only used by dictators of 3rd or 4th World countries - by people who want to absolutely rule and control every source of resistance to a dictator or to a dictator's government. It's just Not Done!

Dictators use this kind of thinking. A dictator uses tactics like these as applied directly to members of the government to control allegiance and totally root out dissidence. When you hear a Head of State yell out at rallies, "lock her up" about someone who ran against him as a candidate - you know that it is absolutely not what is done in any well-run democracy.

We do not lock up our rivals in a Democracy. We do not belittle or abuse our rivals in our Democracy. We do not harass and criminally investigate our rivals in our democracy. This is criminality - a Crime Boss' way of thinking and a war tactic.

It is also used very effectively by autocratic dictators in 3rd World countries. We do not run criminal investigations on people who were just doing the jobs they were elected to do or selected to do by elected officials. You just do not do this to normal law-abiding and functioning citizens - our servants.

Now to the Deep State. What I just said above, leads right into the nonsense about a Deep State. A democracy is based on three branches of government; the judicial, the administrative and the legislative branches, which are equal in stature and authority and have responsibilities to act as a check and balance against the other branches. Particularly used, in this case, for the executive branch or the executive himself.

Part of the stability of this kind of government, a Democracy, is that people are hired into Bureaus, Agencies and offices, such as the FBI and Intelligence, to do various long-term kinds of work, using their skills to protect the nation and its people from Foreign or Domestic crimes or harm. These people are career people. They are there for a very long time by design to be the stable part of the government when politics change. They are the non-political experts who know their job and do their job very well - carrying it out regardless of who the president is or who is in Congress or who's in the Courts. That gives democracy its ultimate stability to operate over long periods independently of the whims of the moment.

So, when a leader at the top of the government starts claiming that people that have been doing their jobs - are committing espionage or being part of a Dark State trying to take down the Resident or the administration or the government - you feel that you may now be living under a dictatorship. No road map. It is just common sense. You just know that. That is Never Done in a democracy such as the United States.

96   So when you hear it, look out! You may have crossed over from a democracy to autocracy. By then, to reverse it may be very, very difficult. Even an election may not be successful at ridding the country of such an entity that has metastasized to that point. Hopefully, we are not at that point quite yet!

Did no one look into this man's background before he ran for office or was Selected? Did no one know the kinds of things he did in business or the kinds of people he was associated with in his business dealings, for example, with Putin before being Selected? Why wouldn't we have done much more Due Diligence as we would have done before selecting a president of a small company in any town in the US? Would we ever consider a con man to be the head of the government of the United States? Would we ever have considered a person with a seemingly full intent to destroy the United States? I mean completely! So much was done, that it seemed that he was well on his way to completing it right before our very eyes?

Every American should've been able to recognize similar behavior from movies they'd seen. The people of America should be able to recognize the characteristics of dictators from other countries. Red flags should have been seen by experts, and they should have warned us this might be someone that may be truly on the wrong path for America. Why isn't there a published road map going into an election which sends up red flags when these things are suspected? When Intelligence experts may have seen these flags, why wasn't an alarm set off immediately? Oh yes, I forgot: many of those experts are the people that are being *investigated right now*!

WITNESS TAMPERING, INTIMIDATION
and MANIPULATION of PROSECUTORS

You say any of these things anywhere near a courtroom in the United States and you're bound to have trouble in a trial - possibly ending in at least a mistrial or a lot of other crimes and offenses that will be thrown at you. None of these things are considered to be petty offenses in a courtroom or a trial of any kind or at any level or stature of a court. This kind of crime is just not taken lightly and quite often deserves quite a number of years of incarceration for just this or similar offenses alone. It often might be associated with gang or organized crime trials.

In a recent trial, those were some of the indictments for which Mr. Stone was found guilty in a federal court. The federal incarceration guidelines apparently were 7 to 9 years for these offenses. The Resident apparently thought they should be much less. Seemingly, the Attorney General stepped in to alter the recommendations to the court to be much less time. Far worse, he had apparently stepped in to try to drop charges against someone who may have committed serious crimes against the state. That person confessed in court at least twice to those crimes and was only awaiting sentencing.

Now I ask you: How does that represent the people's interests for Justice in our federal courts or in the DOJ's office? That same Attorney General recommended that the DOJ should recommend maximum sentences for crimes prosecuted in federal courts. Apparently, the conclusion is that maximum sentences are good enough for Joe Blow but not for friends or buddies of people in high places. Nothing seemed good enough for them even if it might be zero time in jail. What happened to "no one is above the law" in the United States of America?

98   What happened to "equal justice under the law"? What happened to "not being able to buy your way out of a sentence for a crime" even if you had enough money or influence? Apparently, screwing the little guy who doesn't have the money seems to be ok. It would appear that corruption abounds in His administration! If you had believed the swamp was drained, you would've discovered that they had filled it with Alligators.

Every day now, we may be seeing the real results of the Selection of a Resident that was probably the worst possible thing that could happen to America in its entire history. The worst part is that it's not over. The worst part is that we are just now beginning to see how really bad it was and how much worse it could still become if it is not ended by at least one of these myriads of upcoming court actions.

Oh yes, we are not quite through with this chapter. There is this nasty little matter of manipulation of Prosecutors. How independent was this Attorney General that was at the head of our DOJ - the people's Department of Justice? It seemed that we had a very independent group of Justice Prosecutors in DC and a particularly independent group of Prosecutors in the southern district of New York. Both of these groups had been working to investigate a number of people who, in one way or another, were apparently involved in meddling in the election in 2016 or were somehow possibly related to activities in Russia trying to influence the outcome of the 2016 election.

There were apparently 11 or 12 of these cases being investigated as a result of the Mueller investigation into activities related to Russian involvement in the 2016 election. These two prosecuting offices were well known for their total independence and their fairness in evidence collection.

Apparently, this same Attorney General (supposedly the People's Attorney General to provide Equal Justice for the United States) had intervened in these Justice Departments to meddle with those in charge of those investigations in a way that they might have been severely compromised if not totally shut down. It would seem that the outcome of this effort was to bury these and the entire existence of the Mueller report along with Russia's involvement concerning the 2016 election; apparently so that it would no longer be in existence. Finito!

Again, one has only to ask this very basic question. Why was it so damn important to obliterate the very existence of the Mueller report when it presumably had been declared by the Attorney General to exonerate the Resident completely of any involvement with Russia or in its meddling with the 2016 election to favor the selection of this Resident to that office?

Only a guilty person would attempt to try to destroy all evidence of any guilt - and that report has more than enough evidence to adequately justify a strong connection to Russia in the 2016 election. These actions alone seem enough to verify that connection. Why are we not able to do what detectives do with a storyboard? Making connections with strings from one suspect to another to critically show how these groups of people were interconnected to take actions to pull off the Selection of the Resident with the aid of Russian involvement? All of the evidence that was collected by US and international news seemed more effective by far than the Mueller report at connecting the dots. Sadly, that report seemed nearly a total waste of time, money and, in particular, a total waste of two precious years that seriously irritated the Resident and while preventing real progress in discovery and possibly important needed action. That was no way to run an election in the United States of America! NO WAY! NO HOW!

CHAPTER 25
Decent People Being TRANSFORMED

What breadth or depth of mesmerism does it take to convert a decent person into the evil spawning person that HE represents? What does it take to clone a decent person into being a fawning, evil doppelganger, mirror image, lackey of an evil criminal host? It must take a complete alchemy!

In short, throughout these many years, we have seen people, decent people, politicians, people of honor, grace and intelligence, discerning intellects and critically thinking people, seemingly become Jekyll and Hyde. Unfortunately, they seemed to permanently end up as Mr. Hyde. In this role they would remain damned for the rest of their lives. What is worse, seemingly in all of these cases, there is no cure for these transformations. They apparently have become the permanent clones of the master that they seemingly chose to follow.

For the majority of those who have lived in the United States who themselves were decent, discerning people and have known these people before being cloned, they cannot comprehend -- cannot imagine how these people that they have known for decades have become something that they do not recognize; nor can they understand their current behavior.

It all goes well beyond any concept of logic or reasoning. It cannot be described or understood by anything that common, decent people have contemplated, understood, or imagined. How could this happen? How could this happen to anyone?

There's one that is an extreme case in point! He used to have, (for a Republican) liberal views and drew rational conclusions about events whether on national security or political issues or events. He could be counted on to come up with reasonable evaluations of critical situations and be pretty much on the more-sane side of all crisis issues as well as day-to-day policies. One golf game! Just one game and he seemingly became a very irrational, confusing person that we see today.

Every time I see him talk on television in response to a crucial issue, pronouncements or actions that have agitated, I think to myself, does this guy ever look at himself on TV? Does he ever listen to what he's now saying? Would it ever make sense to him? Why is he not horrified, ashamed, besmirched or disgraced by his pronouncements? Look at yourself on television, man! What do you see? Can you actually stand there and not throw a brick at the television set? How can you not be horrified by the very things you are saying totally in the antithesis of your former reasonable self? My God man, get a real life! At least get back to who you were before you were cloned by the former W. H. MAGA GOP body snatcher.

CHAPTER26
Who Were They before EPIPHANY?

The events that had occurred since the acquittal in the impeachment, showed an emboldening of the Resident in ways so completely unimaginable to anybody in America that we must have, by force, cried out in fear for what might be coming next. It seemed so unbelievable! I have only to refer to the chapter of the Resident's visits to Kim and Putin to get a feel of how dire and unimaginable these possibilities could be if possibly tutored by those two rascals. The 'horror' of what might have been achieved by those visits gives us a feel of what I'm just about to discuss.

Who were these people that were once GOP politicians, Congressmen or Senators? Did they grow up pretty much normally but at some time, perhaps in high school, realized that "when I grow up, I want to be a fascist or a Russian Bolshevik"? That's what I really want to be. However, in the meantime until the right person comes along, I'm going to be a politician, a constitutionalist and get elected for those who put me into office to represent their needs for schools, better economies, more available jobs, lower unemployment and all of those great things. I'm going to fight for and pledge to defend the Constitution and defend the rule of law to keep this nation great, safe and most of all - Democratic."

What happens when a person (seemingly a bumbling fool, with no knowledge of or caring about the Constitution and doesn't believe in the rule of law) takes over the minds of these GOP clones as if by a mind warp? I mean, were they latent fascists or anarchists in their subconscious youths? Did they have deep, hidden dispositions to be this kind of odd minded GOP?

The Resident seemingly didn't believe that he needed the Congress or the Courts - except to sue people. Why is it that these people, who presumably at one time grew up (as the rest of us did) believing in the Constitution, the rule of law, a democratic way of life, suddenly choose to take this different path? How could it have happened, when they lived in a place that was run by the rule of law that insured, to the best of its ability, peace, tranquility and prosperity?

Why now are they seemingly all acting as if somewhere in their deep dark past and dreams they had really wanted to be Fascists that wanted to take over our rule of law Democracy? After their families and they have lived here, perhaps, for generations - why might they suddenly be inclined to want to turn it into a Russian style dictatorship: requiring total loyalty to ONE as the only means of keeping their jobs? Why be in an environment where if one steps out of line - somebody else, who may be far worse, steps in?

My first question is "where in hell do they find the next person that could be worse?" Where do *they* come from? What country did they live in before they were so dissatisfied with the rule of law and the Constitution that they were so eager to give it all up and join this seemingly pure form of insanity?

Where? Where in hell would anybody, after a normal time in grade school, high school or college and into politics, have latent tendencies to be fascists or Bolsheviks just waiting to come out? I can't understand how these people can suddenly have such an awful, awful epiphany and seemingly embrace it as if this is what they always wanted to be all their lives! I don't think so. OMG! They have children who know better. They have grandchildren who know better! Where in Hell have they been hiding? Where in Hell have these alter egos been hiding?

104   Where were those in the 40's, when fascism rose to power, that suddenly arose to do the bidding and dirty work? It is said that every deviant, derelict, dysfunctional sociopath in society was ready to join and be part of the government. Apparently, in every society, there must be some sort of bell curve of behaviors and at the very bottom of the bell curve are the scum of the earth: the totally out-of-sorts people with deep, hidden grudges against Society. How did they survive before?

They were people without morals - with no moral code whatsoever. They had no empathy for anyone, they were total societal misfits; barely surviving within a normal functioning democracy. These people are relegated to the dark corners of humanity hidden away and minimized and marginalized to the point where they just barely existed.

What happened was that these people were found and given not only Authority but Power; all that they wanted. That is all they needed to come forth and do whatever they felt like doing because they could not only get by with it and be rewarded for it; they could do no wrong. They had been given a free hand to be the meanest bastards you would ever want to meet. The meaner they were the better, because by being a mean bastard they struck fear into normal people's hearts. It was such a dark fear that if you didn't fall in line you'd be killed. There was no other alternative. Lives to them were of no consequence!

Well, the last six years have shown us that we may be at that point now in America. If you were going to be part of this man's government you had to absolutely swear an oath but not to the United States or to the Constitution. If you had the misfortune to work in this government and you fell out of line, you might be toast. In your job if you happened to tell the truth and it wasn't liked, you may no longer have your job. Worse yet, you might be persecuted or prosecuted. You might have been called a criminal against the State - a traitor that may have committed treason.

You may be identified as part of the Deep State - planted there by the previous occupiers so that they could help destroy the new kingdom. It is just damn hard to fathom how any person could just become one of those sycophants that just seemed to be so overly supportive of this regime. Where's the soul?

We needed to know so much more in the beginning, things not familiar to us in America, to be able to see the future. In history, it's often been shown that early knowledge was mandatory in order to mitigate possibly portending situations. There is no surprise that someone who might be, for whatever reason, trying to pull a fast one over the public, would do all they could to keep it absolutely secret and out of sight. Unfortunately, too many of us ignored prior history and didn't see what was happening as the result of his ever-present quirky behavior. Abundant hidden evidence became clear only too late for us to be able to do much prevention or remediation.

Eventually, it became clear that you could see definite things through the smoke screen that were very disturbing. Clear indications were there, several years ago, that we should have seen and taken swift action to mitigate. Some of this had happened within the virus pandemic that we are still fighting. Some didn't pay attention to known facts and virus dynamics. Instead of swift action, they seemed prone to slow foot dragging. There are so many dire lessons that we all learned far too late - that we must seriously heed in the future. Some of them are examples of asymmetric warfare that have been revealed in the last 10 chapters. We've so much more to learn!

CHAPTER 27
ELITISM, LAISSEZ-FAIRE and VIGILANTISM,

Elitism: the advocacy or existence of an elite as a dominating element in a system or society. The attitude or behavior of a person and/or a group who regard themselves as belonging to an elite. Further is the belief or attitude that individuals who form an elite, a select group of people with an intrinsic quality, high intellect, wealth, special skills or experience, are more likely to be constructive to society as a whole, and therefore deserve influence or authority greater than that of the others. The term elitism may be used to describe a situation in which power is concentrated in the hands of a limited number of people. Elite theory opposes:

Pluralism: (more than one system of power). A tradition that assumes that all individuals, or at least the multitude of social groups, have equal power and balance each other out in contributing to democratic political outcomes representing the emergent, aggregate will of society.

Laissez-faire: A policy or attitude of letting things take their own course without interfering. Abstention by governments from interfering in the workings of the free market. It means letting people do what they choose. It describes a system or point of view that opposes regulation or interference by the government in economic affairs beyond the minimum necessary to allow the free enterprise system to operate according to its own laws.

Vigilantism: is law enforcement undertaken without legal authority by a self-appointed group of people. A vigilante justice, as defined by The Legal Information Institute, is the actions of a single person or group of people who claim to enforce the law but lack the legal authority to do so.

Vigilantism itself is not illegal under US law, however it offense involves actions that are often Illegal.

Wondering why these definitions are at the start of this chapter? It's an interesting thing but it reflects on confusing aspects of what we've experienced in the last 6 years. They're somewhat orthogonal to each other - yet somehow have been combined in a strange mix of conflicting intents and practices.

Elitism was what the head of that government thought he was for those past 4 years. He thought he was smarter, better, more knowledgeable and more capable than anybody ever could be - ever, ever! And yet, most thinking people have realized that it's not that at all but just might be quite the opposite. Nonetheless, that is a behavior that seemed to have been imposed upon the United States from 2016 to 2020.

So now: laissez faire is where we are taking off every regulation possible on business, environment and all of the things that have been established to try to make our lives safe and livable - such as clean air, water, our environment, food and drugs. This includes letting business do whatever it wants to take as much money as it wants and therefore to become the best friends of big business and big money.

We see vigilantism begin to creep more into our Petty Pace day-by-day - when people with differences of opinion that feel a need to discuss them in a way that could lead to the greater good - are finding themselves on enemy lists or Blacklists that seem to be targets for governmental investigations and various other means for retaliation. We call COVID 19 the Chinese Virus and suddenly a large number of natural Chinese and Asian citizens are attacked and harassed. The names for this kind of government are very, very ugly.

CHAPTER 28
SVENGALI, ROBESPIERRE and F. A. MESMER

These are very interesting early personages that all have some bearing upon some of the ideas developed in this book. I added them here for your brief intermission, a respite and a very hearty retrospection and personal reflection.

Svengali is a fictional character in George du Maurier's 1895 novel <u>Trilby</u>. Svengali is a musician who seduces, dominates and exploits Trilby, a young Irish girl and makes her a famous singer.

The word Svengali has come to refer to a person who, with evil intent, dominates, manipulates and controls another. In court, a Svengali defense is a legal tactic that purports the defendant to be a pawn in the scheme of a greater and more influential criminal mastermind.

F. A. MESMER A therapeutic system of healing by Mesmer - a technique to induce a trance. Mesmer was a person who used an induced trance to control or have mesmeric influence on another, possibly for a sinister purpose. See e.g. 'mesmerize'.

Maximilian Robespierre: Often quoted Quotes. These are very enlightening and very interesting to read. I very much think that they will play in your mind as applied to this book.

*A nation is truly corrupted when having lost its character and its liberty, passes from democracy to aristocracy or to monarchy. That is the decrepitude and death of the body politic...
*The Secret of Freedom lies in educating people, whereas the secret of tyranny is in keeping them ignorant.
*The king must die so that the country can live.

*To punish the oppressors of humanity is clemency; to forgive them is cruelty.

*Again, it may be said that to love justice and equality the people need no great effort for virtue; it is sufficient that they love themselves.

*Any institution which does not suppose the people are good, and the magistrate corruptible, is evil.

*The general 'will' rules in society as the private 'will' governs each individual.

*Crime butcher's innocence to secure a throne, and innocence struggles with all its might against the attempts of crime.

*Atheism is aristocratic; the idea of a great Being that watches over oppressed innocence and punishes triumphant crime is altogether popular.

*Any law which violates the inalienable rights of man is essentially unjust and tyrannical; it is not a law at all.

*Softness to Traitors will destroy us all.

*People do not judge in the same way as courts of law; they do not hand down sentences, they throw thunderbolts; they do not condemn Kings, they drop them back into the void; and this justice is worth just as much as that of the courts.

*One can... never create freedom by an invading force.

*We must smother the internal and external enemies of the Republic or perish with it; now in this situation, the first maxim of our policy ought to be to lead the People by reason and the People's enemies by terror.

*Smuggle out the truth, pass it through all the obstacles that its enemies fabricate; multiply, spread by all means possible her message so that she may triumph

*Through zeal and civic action - counterbalance the influence of money and the machinations lavished on the propagation of deception. That, in my opinion, is the most useful activity in the most sacred duty of pure patriotism.

110 *Men of all countries are brothers, and the different people should help one another to the best of their ability, like citizens of the same state.

*It is in time of war that the executive power displays the most redoubtable energy and that it wields a sort of dictatorship most ominous to a nascent Liberty...

*War is always the first object of a powerful government which wishes to increase its power. I shall not speak to you of the opportunity that a war affords for a government to exhaust the people and to dissipate its treasure and to cover with an impenetrable veil its depredations and its errors...

*Equality of Rights is established by Nature; Society, far from impairing it, guarantees it against the abuse of power which renders it illusory.

*The people ask only for what is necessary, it only wants justice and tranquility. The rich aspire to everything, they want to invade and dominate everything.

*Abuses are the work and the domain of the rich, they are the scourges of the people: the interest of the people is the general interest, that of the rich is a particular interest.

*It has been said that terror is the principle of despotic government. Does your government therefore resemble despotism?

*Yes, as the sword that gleams in the hands of the heroes of Liberty resembles that with which the henchmen of tyranny are armed.

*I utter this deadly truth with regret, but Louis must die, because the homeland must live.

*The most extravagant idea that can be born in the head of a political thinker is to believe that it suffices for people to enter, weapons in hand, among a foreign people and expect to have its laws and constitution embraced. No one loves armed missionaries; the first lesson of nature and prudence is to repulse them as enemies.

*In every country where nature provides for the needs of   111 men with prodigality, scarcity can only be imputed to defects of administration or of the laws themselves; bad laws and bad administration have their origins in false principles and bad morals.

*The right to punish the tyrant and the right to dethrone him are the same thing; both include the same forms. The tyrant's trial is the insurrection; the verdict, the collapse of his power; the sentence, whatever the liberty of the people requires.

*Happily, virtue is natural in the people, despite aristocratic prejudices.

*We wish, in a word, to fulfill the intentions of nature and the destiny of man, realize the promises of philosophy, and I acquit providences of a long reign of crime and tyranny.

*So that France may become the model for all nations, the terror of oppressors, the consolation of the oppressed. That is our ambition, that is our goal.

*Citizens, did you want a revolution without Revolution?

*Food that is necessary for man's existence is as sacred as life itself. Everything that is indispensable for its preservation is the common property of society as a whole. It is only the surplus that is private property and can be safely left to individual commercial enterprises.

*What is a person who, among men equal in rights, dares to declare his fellows unworthy of theirs, and to take them away for his own advantage! Amen. We sure understand this one!

There is just so much in these - complete, brilliant wisdom in all of his quotes that - written during the French Revolution - have so much to bear on our present situation and issues. I sincerely hope that you all perceived the poignancy of sheer knowledge displayed in these simple short pearls of wisdom. In a very real sense these condensed thoughts were written in similar times and during periods of similar stressful actions.

Before the final steps of publishing this book I awoke from my sleep with the essence of an epilogue to summarize what I had discovered while writing the book. All of these varied chapters suddenly coalesced into one conglomerate - a very profound thought (perhaps a synopsis).

We found ourselves in a horrible global pandemic of a brand new virus to which no one was immune. This is so dangerous that, like the 1918 Spanish Flu, a significant part of the world population would die - 3% to 5% - if not mitigated by as swift, decisive and effective actions as possible.   The Bubonic Plague deaths were estimated at 30% to 60% of the world population. They knew so much less about such things then.

The Epiphany, as revealed by the summation of the book, was in effect, a different kind of global pandemic that appears to be sweeping many parts of the world today. We have seen its essence in the recent elections in the EU, France, England (with Brexit), Turkey, Italy, etc. Nationalist movements, such as those sweeping Europe, such as Marine Le Pen, winning with 24% over Macron's 21% in France. This Populist, Nationalist, Progressive movement seemingly is more prevalent now here, just as in other parts of the world. While fascism is often rooted in Populism it doesn't mean that Populism always ends in fascism.

As stated earlier, a viral pandemic acts like an atomic bomb - a basic chain reaction. The bomb occurs in milliseconds. The viral pandemic (much slower) takes a few to many months to play out - at least the first time. The Nationalist Populism pandemic, however, plays out over a period of several years. Boron absorbers can slow the reaction in the atomic reactor - while distancing is most important to slow a viral pandemic.

So what is available to slow the onslaught of the Populist, Nationalist, Progressive worldwide movements? First of all, these are ideology driven - not inanimate objects like Uranium atoms or viruses. Neither of those two have minds or can think or remember prior events or be convinced of or imagine other circumstances. As a result, they tend to follow laws of physics or human nature.

The latter can only be influenced by words - i.e., education, propaganda or verbal persuasion of the mind and emotions. These radical ideas just seem to be so counterintuitive to common sense, basic human needs and desires, that little to nothing could possibly overwhelm them. However, lies, false words - propaganda are very effective at overcoming these natural instincts. That is what makes this pandemic so very dangerous - when even human instincts and common sense can be overwhelmed. So how can one slow or stop such a dangerous runaway train? There-in lies the "fight to control human minds". Lies, fake news, alternate truths, deceit and propaganda are the main causes of these kinds of movements. Kitsch, catchy slogans appeal to an ad hoc patriotism. Simple phrases (like Lock her up, build the wall, who will pay for it?) that can be easily remembered and chanted - all add to a cohesiveness leading to a kind of cultism which might be similar to 'Jonestown'. I'm patiently waiting for my "Kool-Aid". When do we get our "Kool-Aid", please?

The moderator to this kind of chain reaction? That's a hard one. Since words - primarily LIES - are the propagators - then it must be words - THE TRUTH - that has to be used to slow it down or possibly reverse it. But how do you force THE TRUTH into closed minds? How do you find a crack into the psyche of a cultist member? I've tried to find answers in the literature and found it sadly bereft. Could it be pervasive truth checking?

114   Often much of what has spurred the rise of Nationalism Is an apparent mistrust of liberal thinking parties that have seemingly abandoned the working class in favor of Wall Street over Main Street. In effect, they seem to have offered little for ordinary working people and have failed to mitigate rapidly increasing inequality. The rich get richer while the poor get poorer. So, the simplest methods to counter or diminish Nationalism seems to be to promote a progressive agenda that would definitely side with working people again.

Those 70,000 votes that Selected the one in the White House were from typically liberal leaning (known as rust belt) states that apparently may have felt ignored by the Liberal Party. They expressed their possible anger in a protest vote against the usual party by voting for someone who often chided them with: "What have you got to lose?" and adding a catchy phrase of "Making America Great Again" (typically a Nationalist kind of sentiment). This works, especially, for those who may have seriously felt left behind by their historically supportive party!

We must counter incredibly ineffective, flawed, administrations that seemed to think like a rogue 10K marathon runner. He started the race with the others, then ducked out and caught a ride to the finish line neighborhood and jumped out in front of those dedicated, hardworking, disciplined racers to cross the finish line just before them. That is equivalent to doing nothing during the 2 most critical months of the virus. Then, only after the nation's governors, out of necessity, had done all that they could to mitigate it, stepped in and asserted that he and the federal government had been heroic in fighting this virus! What a total pile of BS!

To counter this kind of Nationalistic bullshit is simply TRUTH and progressive agendas to benefit the forgotten workers.

Oh, my God: oh, my GOD! All of the muted and subtle warnings that I made in this book were just about to be sent to the publisher when things happened that would make the rule of law, Constitution-defending Democratic citizen's minds literally explode! So much so that I had to add at least thirteen more pages to this book as a dire warning that must be heeded as soon as possible. Everyone with a conscience must act NOW!

Large groups of Constitution, rule of law and democracy - minded people cannot afford to idly talk about aspirations any more. They must immediately get together to form groups or institutions that will formulate and take decisive actions now. We can no longer 'pray for the families of Sandy Hook kids' and do nothing! The time has come for serious intervention and dire mitigation on a scale no less important than the one that should have been put in place for this world-threatening pandemic. We can no longer pray for something to happen; real urgent action must be taken now to save this Nation - especially before the election. That's how bad things were, and they are very rapidly moving to become far WORSE!

Way too often I heard news people and especially politicians, utter "Well, this is awful; somebody should do something" or, "Oh, that's just the way he is!" NO! Never EVER under any circumstances do you make excuses or allowances for bad, totally destructive behavior. I don't give a DAMN who he is!

Let's review steps often taken by a would-be autocrat hell bent upon the gradual takeover of a well-running democracy.

1. Obliterate the validity of the free press and news media - that had been the first fundamental necessary part of a democracy or just take it over or censure it thoroughly.

2. Replace the Head of the DOJ with a person who is totally loyal and that will effectively weaponized it against your opponents or perceived enemies and will do everything to encourage the end of the rule of law. Your loyalists!

3. Stack the courts with loyalist cronies who may not even be real or effective judges. In effect, they may have taken loyalty oaths to you. This is by far the most anti-Democratic thing that you can do. This is never, ever done in a functioning Democracy!

4. Always Lie! This way no one can ever convict you based upon facts said! When based upon Lies - America dies!

5. Stack (or convert) the house that is responsible for approving all of your appointees (including judges) with people that will block all of the People's legislation and approve of only your hand-picked laws and expressions.

6. Fill all cabinet positions with hand-picked Department Cronies that will do your bidding to administratively demolish the real effectiveness of those administrations from protecting your bosses, i.e. the American citizens, from polluted water, air and environments - bad food or drugs - homeland security - pestilence, plagues and wars.

7. Pick a Secretary of State whose agenda is foremost to look out for your own financial, business and political interests - and thereby act upon them on your behalf and to your favor. This is just not done in a Democracy.

8. Censure all scientists from crucial areas affecting the ultimate wellbeing of the people such as in health, economics, climate change or environmental issues.

9. Remove all Inspector Generals that may or do have jurisdiction over possible acts of corruption or law that may affect you or your Cronies directly.

Look at these. Are we not already in deep Doo Doo? Act Now!

The United States and the entire world, find ourselves trying to fight and survive one of the deadliest worldwide viral pandemics in over 100 years - since the 1918 Spanish Flu. In this severe crisis when it would be expected that our Federal Government would have mobilized to do everything that was possible to save our nation from getting infected or more importantly to prevent unneeded deaths - we appear to have come up woefully lacking by apparently foot dragging.

Where "*expected to serve*" is the norm, the opposite seems to be the intent. Where the immediate financial needs of an entire vulnerable population are paramount; huge corporations and the rich seem to be highly served to the detriment of the most vulnerable. When the most vulnerable are at risk: retirement communities, prisons, high density food processing plants and minority people and neighborhoods seem to have the highest infection rates and densities and seem to be served the least of all (seemingly deliberately ignored and forgotten)!

Most disturbing of all is that during this extremely serious crisis we found, apparently purposeful foot dragging and much of what's been depicted in 1. to 9. above, apparently going on in the background with deliberate intent.

Not to diminish its import or impact, we, as a nation, seem to now have faux militias storming into our state legislative houses and chambers armed with automatic long guns and intimidating legislators and spectators. This only happens in autocratic third world countries (never in the very beacon of Democracy, the United States of America). Where are those constitutionalists that, till now, have so fervently defended the precepts of the Constitution and the rule of law? Is this not understood to be what happens near the end of a democracy such as in Europe in the '30s? Are we not already there?

THE VERY FOREBODING BOTTOM LINE
            This is so Important it should be the Preface

We just "survived" a very anxious and ominous mid-term election. Traditionally, the party in power is expected to be over-run by a "Tidal Wave" that reverses who controls the House and the Senate. The Republican party had 300 "Election Deniers" running for crucial offices in over 30 states. These would have been Governors, Congressmen, District Attorneys, Secretaries of State and heads of election boards for the States as well as controlling numbers of Legislatures. They could control gerrymandering of voting districts in the States and pass very restrictive voting laws that essentially would by-pass the will of the voters. If the traditionally predicted "Red Tidal Wave" had occurred, the Democrats would have lost control of the Senate and had a huge reversal of the majority in the House of Representatives. A majority of states might have ended up being controlled by "election deniers"; this would have put America squarely on the fast track to becoming a Fascist Autocratic Dictatorship. (FAD)

Thankfully, instead of the "Red Wave" we were spared almost everything except a very small GOP majority in the House of Representatives. We all gave a very thankful sigh of relief because the Fascist Autocratic Dictatorship had seemingly been averted - for now! We all felt so much better prepared for winning the election in 2024. The Devil had seemingly been rejected by the American Public. Now, perhaps, we could get on with actually passing legislation that would be beneficial for America. Unfortunately, this little midterm election skirmish was but a diversion to get attention away from the real danger that had been steadily growing in America for at least the past eight years. Very terrible ominous events were just about to make it abundantly clear to us that we were not out of danger.

Within days, the new leadership of the House announced that they were not going to cooperate with the minority of the House; but instead would start a large onslaught of vengeful investigations into members of the Democratic Party (including impeachment proceedings against President Biden, Nancy Pelosi and Anthony Fauci). Apparently, this was supposed to get the voters back that had abandoned them in the midterms. Go figure! Does any of that make any sense to you? It defeats all wisdom of how to win back voters. Oh, now I remember. We were talking about Asymmetrical Warfare. It's about breaking all of the rules and doing everything that goes counter to normal reasoning and expectations. It also belies the belief that, in the future, they will not have to worry about what the voter may think, because they will be ruling as a dictatorship.

Now, if you thought that was bad, look out; it gets much worse! A week ago, the ex-President had dinner at Mar-a-Lago with Kanye West and a hate-spewing White Supremacist. This last one would make Hitler look like a saint by comparison. The ex- President "claimed" that he did not know anything about this hateful White Supremacist. That kind of convenient denial is an old habit of the ex-President. Then, as if to put a very fine point on it, Kanye West spent hours on Alex Jones' Infowars Show proclaiming how wonderful Hitler was. He also spread hate toward the Jewish people. This seemed to create a touchy moment for those in the MAGA GOP party. However, hate crimes against those of the Jewish and Muslim faiths have had a very sudden increase since all of this Anti-Semitism talk has increased on the propaganda platforms. It seems to be openly and deliberately propagated by members of the MAGA GOP party. Maria Ressa's new book; <u>How to Stand Up to a Dictator</u>, warns, very clearly, how dangerous these seemingly one-off events tend to be steps toward taking down a Democracy and replacing it with a Fascist . (FAD)

120   Let me interject some extremely important facts of nature here. There is an absolute law of nature described in physics. It is called the Second Law of Thermodynamics and is about a term called Entropy. Entropy increases as a measure of disorder. The law states that in nature, the world or the universe, Entropy always increases or stays the same. Reduced to terms that most people can understand, all things, if left alone without help or intervention, will decay to disorder. For example, it is far easier to destroy a skyscraper than to plan it, build it and maintain it. It was far easier to destroy the NY Trade Center buildings on 911 than to plan them and build them. It is far easier to destroy apartments and people's lives in Ukraine with missiles and high explosives than it is to create those buildings and hundreds of lives. It is far easier to destroy the lives of 19 children in a school in Uvalde with an AR-15 than it has been to create, nurture and grow those 19 children. Are you getting the point of this exercise in Asymmetric warfare?

It's thousands of times easier to destroy things of value than it is to build them and maintain them. Likewise, it's thousands of times easier to destroy the lives and reputations of others than it is to build them. Just one false word, one deliberate lie, one tweet on the internet is all that it takes to ruin the life or reputation of a person that took years to build. In general, people are very proud of their achievements and hard-fought accomplishments. They should never be proud of deliberately destroying something of immense value such as a company like Twitter. Destruction of this company, which took years and thousands of people to build, is certainly nothing to be proud of. Especially when you use ineptness to do it in just a matter of six weeks! The point: millions of people who built America in 240 years and it was almost destroyed in just 4 years by a few very determined Fascist Terrorists using Asymmetric Weaponry!

What does it mean that everything of value, requiring years of planning, funding and hard work to build, can be destroyed in a matter of minutes with an asymmetric weapon such as a missile or simple explosives? What does it mean that a person's entire life of endeavor and worth can be terminated in a second with a gun? What does it mean that this can be done even faster and on a much larger scale with weapons such as AR-15s.? The law of Entropy shows that anything of worth can be easily destroyed by totally inept persons in an instant, but that things of worth can only be built by many, many very skilled and hard-working individuals over a very long period of time. The law basically says that it takes a lot of energy to construct anything of value, but because of the fact that Entropy always increases, it takes almost nothing to destroy anything of value. THIS is the BASIS of any war using ASYMMETRIC WEAPONS and is the BASIS of ALL TYRANNY!

OK, does that mean that Entropy has now created two distinct classes of people in the world? The bulk of the world, hopefully, thrives upon doing very worthwhile things for humanity and for the betterment of everyone's way of life. Many do it out of love for their work and efforts, and perhaps to achieve fame and possibly fortune as the result of the love of their work. They do great things and can be proud of their accomplishments - even if they are not rewarded publicly! These people spent years in apprenticeships, education and training in order to achieve great things, often in cooperation with many other dedicated people with equivalent training and experience in a variety of fields. The other, hopefully much smaller, segment tends to think that the world owes them a living, fame and fortune. As a result, they are the grifters, con-men, charlatans, thieves, robbers, carpetbaggers and often Narcissists! They want it all without having to do any work!

122   They think that they can run a company, or a Nation; and all that is needed is to be called a manager or a President. They don't feel that they need to train for the job or to have a great deal of experience before taking the position. They think that if there is an easy way to obtain fame or fortune, then that should be their way of life. They are always looking for the short cut, the easy way out or the perpetual motion machine. They think that they deserve a free lunch or that the world owes them a living - a very rich and powerful living! And how can you obtain that "perpetual motion machine"? Ah, by using asymmetric weapons to get the things you want very quickly!

So, let's break down humanity. Those that have a soul, a sense of self-worth added to a sense of compassion, constantly strive to better themselves in every way and to dedicate their lives to hard work, training, experience and endeavors to do things of value for not only themselves but for the world as well. Inventors find problems that have plagued a large number of people and then strive to solve them in some way or another. Highly trained scientists work to ease medical ailments by developing new miracle drugs. Politicians get elected to go to Congress to work for the good of the people of the Nation. They take a solemn oath to defend the Constitution before taking their roles in Congress. The President does that as well.

What happens when a person who loves "perpetual motion machines" runs for public office? He is not interested in doing any work for the job and actually has no desire to legislate or to pass any laws. He could be called an obstructionist. He is likely to be one whose entire goal is to disrupt everything good about the purposes of such an institution. The problem quite often manifests itself into being someone who desires to tear down everything that makes sense to the majority of society.

His interests are probably using the job to make a lot of quick money or, worse yet, to gain an extraordinary amount of power and control over not only the institution but the Nation itself. If you are just such a person, you are likely to be hell-bent upon tearing everything down, including the Constitution, the Rule of Law and every tradition that makes the country great. What is the fastest way to do that? Entropy taught us how to use asymmetric warfare to break down and destroy everything of value in the shortest possible time. Above all, it doesn't require much training or knowledge to accomplish the worst possible outcomes in the shortest amount of time while expending the least amount of energy to do it. You can intimidate an awful lot of people into doing almost anything that you want very quickly with guns or faux militias.

These people want quick, low energy cost outcomes. They don't care about the consequences for people. They seek recognition, wealth and power without earning it. They tend to be shallow, empathy deprived, totally uncaring and probably Narcissistic people. They can't be shamed, embarrassed and are definitely not introspective. They tend to become total Pariahs. The worst part of how well asymmetric work is that they are NOT tactics that the opposition would ever think of using and are definitely not tactics that they would ever use. Sane people tend to think that everyone else is a reasonable person. That fact alone, is what makes this kind of asymmetric weapon so powerful. People want a comfortable trouble-free life. For a person that is willing to be disciplined enough to not let that kind of discomfort bother them, it allows them to quickly and easily get the upper hand in most situations. The general public during the rise of Hitler did the best that they could to ignore and survive the best way that they could during the worst possible times under the Gestapo. They simply kept their heads down and did nothing to provoke anyone.

124   The result of this warfare is that the MAGA GOP end up looking like they have lost their bloody minds! If they stand for anything, it is being against everything that might be beneficial to the citizens of the United States. Instead, they are hell-bent upon revenge in all forms against everyone that they consider to be their enemies. It doesn't matter if they can't construct a valid cause to make the case. They will invent one because it is the SPECTACLE of revenge that is the most important part of that form of asymmetric warfare. (Debord, Guy (2021). *The Society of Spectacle.* Critical Editions) The public display of false grievances creates a propaganda spectacle that is used to destroy the best images of any opposition. It is used to degrade someone before they are able to define themselves in a better light. They will malign family members as well so that it reflects badly upon the integrity of the intended target.

So why aren't they concerned about "doing the right thing" for the public good instead of this irresponsible use of public power to destroy every one of their perceived enemies?

No. 1: they have no intention of ever having an election in the future that has any consequences. They intend to abide by a rule, of their making, that elections are only just and fair when they win and are totally corrupt and fraudulent when they lose. They ignore the obvious flaw that occurs when some of the GOP candidates win in the same election that others lose. "That inconsistency is just the hobgoblin of small minds".

No. 2: It is far more important to them to run against a totally damaged candidate in a valid election than it is to run against a solid, popular one. See what happened to Hillary Clinton with the email server in her basement and the Benghazi hearings. When they added a "cherry on top" of her "being untrustworthy, dishonest and unlikeable" they had a perfect storm to defeat her in the most valid of any elections. It's not just this apparent insanity of the MAGA GOP to go

totally against all common sense of humanity by taking
actions that normally would tank most candidates. This is
especially so when they have just seen how poorly that kind of
candidate fared in the 2022 midterm elections. That should
have been a very strong message to try to do better. It is the
fact that they are betting on that being a winning strategy that
is the most puzzling. Even more puzzling is that they continue
to take this "running lemmings", "pied piper" self-annihilation
path to such extremes that they would end up destroying, not
just their chances of winning elections, but additionally, the
entire society, government, Nation and the Constitution as
well.

It isn't what we see coming out of Mar-a-Lago with the Racist,
White Supremacists, Nazi sympathizers and Hitler worshipers
that is the most worrisome.   It is all of the very silent, slowly
moving, behind the scenes actions that are happening in small
towns and communities in almost every state in the union.   It
is a clandestine war to destroy freedom of speech, religion
and choice. It is the local asymmetric war on school boards,
courts, libraries, voting boards and most other civic
associations that may play a role in deleteriously altering
standards and norms of behaviors as well as normalizing
harmful mores. Even if we are successful at eventually voting
this Cancer out of office on the National scale and throwing as
many of them as is possible into jail, we will still be left with
this widespread cultural cancer throughout our entire society.
It will be, in effect, the "silent dark state" left behind to torment
the rest of America, perhaps, for generations to come. It will
also be the "lievito madre" or "Mother starter" used to spawn
off destructive movements and factions in the future when
called upon by fomenters of future Fascist Autocratic
Dictatorships (FAD). Faux militias will also be part of the
underground left to wage intimidation and harassment when
needed to kick ass.

126   So much of this last part is the most troubling for me. It's been two years since Treason was committed in the Capitol on 1/6/21. For those years the justice department sat on their hands and apparently did essentially nothing to investigate, detain or arrest any of the top-tier planners and perpetrators. Do you know how much damage an organized group of domestic terrorists can do in just a month, let alone two years? So many arrests should have been made within the first three months after 1/6/21. It was known since 1/6/21 that not just the White House but more than one hundred Congressmen were directly involved or sympathized with the goals of the Insurrection in the Capitol. At the very least, they should have been required to renew their Oaths taken to defend the Constitution or be immediately terminated from their duties in Congress. What good is an oath required to perform your work if it means absolutely nothing in practice? Is it only a sham?!

There are those eighty-four people in seven states that met in December 2020 to sign fraudulent documents to certify that they were the authorized alternate electors for the Electoral College to vote for Trump to be President of the United States. They all signed bogus documents that were sent by mail to the Senate and the National Archives. That is called mail fraud and is a very serious Federal crime. It should have been an easy solution to use the United States Postal Inspection Service (or Postal Inspectors) to file mail fraud charges against all eighty - four of those false electors. Why did we delay this action that could have been done as soon as it was discovered?

When it comes to the Treasonous Insurrection in the Capitol on 1/6/21 there is only one person in the world that would benefit from planning and instigating that serious crime and there's only one person crazy enough to even think of doing it.

Even images that were taken at the White House while
the mob was battering down the windows and doors of the Capitol, besieging the offices of prominent Congressmen, desecrating the seat of our government, showed us how pleased that one person was that this medieval onslaught was progressing so well. The fact that he seemed pleased and did absolutely nothing to stop the mob for more than three hours proved that he was very much involved in its planning and Instigation.

In contrast, just recently, a planned coup in Germany was stopped before it materialized when 25 conspiracy members were arrested and incarcerated. A possible coup was immediately averted in Peru by an arrest of the president, who tried to close Congress and intended to rule by decree while reforming the country's Constitutional Court and Judiciary. I'm not saying that this might have been possible here in the United States, but the comparison seems to indicate that far more drastic measures needed to be done long before two years after the coup attempt on 1/6/21. The danger is that there is only one message that is understood by Insurrectionists and that is immediate incarceration! Otherwise, they effectively use the advantage of being free to continue their planning and propagandizing very publicly, with what appears to be a total immunity from justice. It falsely lends legitimacy to their cause that is absolutely not deserved and allows them to commit even more heinous grievances against Democracy.

It took the House Select January 6th Committee five months to form and another month to get started. In the following seventeen months they did magnificent work collecting documents and hearing the testimonies of more than a thousand witnesses, but they are not the Justice department. They had no basis to subpoena or to convict anyone. Damn it!

128   Where was the Attorney General or the Department of Justice for those twenty-three months? With crimes as serious as Treason or Insurrection (Constitution and Section 3 of the 14th amendment), there was an urgent need for the survival of our Democracy to get to the source of it within a month or two and then confine more than a couple of hundred planners and perpetrators. A Democracy cannot survive if this kind of Tyranny and insurrection is allowed to fester and thrive. One must look at the terrible history of the rise of Hitler and Nazism in Germany in the 30's and early 40's. Historians have well documented the things that the Weimar government should have done to stop that progression very early in its sequence.

That would have involved early incarceration of hate groups, faux militias, insurrection planners and instigators. It would also include vigorously defending such institutions and principles as freedom of speech and freedom of the press. Censorship and book-burnings should have been met with harsh actions and punishments as soon as they became evident. Separation of Church and State in law should have been defended to avoid the kind of creeping misinterpretations that we are now experiencing in both State Governments and now the Supreme Court.

All expressions of racial or religious discrimination must be treated as not only hate crimes but as a form of intimidation. We can't survive as a Democracy if all we do is have a good economy, low unemployment, and hold inflation in check. We must be actively monitoring the underlying trends and societal structures that are being rapidly altered by groups that have full intentions of eventually taking over the Government and creating a Fascist Autocratic Dictatorship (FAD). Some are religiously inspired to create a Theocratic Dictatorship.

With the House of Representatives being under a slight MAGA GOP majority in 2023, our Democracy will be attacked by the most heinous underbelly of society imaginable. The small majority ensures that the person who desperately wants to be the Speaker will have to make deals with some of the most despicable people on earth. These people have no respect for the purpose of a governing body other than a means to acquire incredible power over the entire government of the United States. Their only idea of legislation surrounds the concept of revenge against everyone else but them. This will take the form of having a plethora of investigative hearings into the lives and dealings of every "boogeyman" Democrat with whom they can create an issue. None of them will have merit, but the SPECTACLE is the thing as an asymmetric war!

The entire MAGA party has become filled with "the scum of the earth," much as Hitler was able to find and recruit every deviant and derelict into his inner circle, the SS and the Gestapo. The meaner, crueler, and inhumane they were, the better! Not only will the House be doing nothing but hate filled hearings, but the MAGA Governors will be establishing faux police forces and investigative boards to harass their citizens and to investigate things like pharmaceutical companies that have rapidly made vaccines to dramatically reduce the deaths from the deadly Covid 19 virus and its mutations. These faux police forces are acting like the Iranian Morality Police that caused a nation-wide demonstration in Iran because it was so brutal. These kinds of actions can only be explained in the context of being a part of a Fascist Autocratic Dictatorship (FAD) that has been established by the Governors of those States. There's no better example of the blatant use of asymmetric warfare tactics than this. Even tremendous successes by the liberals to make people's lives better will not be enough to kill this cancer!

130   Oh, my God! Apparently, Trump has just stated that the Constitution should be terminated because the action taken on 1/6/21 was a legal response to the opposing party attempting massive election fraud. "It was a patriotic act to save America." He is finally saying out loud what he covertly has been doing since 2014 or 2015. He is validating all of those years with overt actions such as having dinner with avid White Supremacists and Fascist sympathizers. He has also failed to condemn either of those attendees, the things they have said, or any of their outspoken beliefs. He has basically verified to the world that he has been and will continue to use asymmetric warfare to destroy America while obtaining absolute power and economic influence over all of the people of America. It is too bad that no one paid any real attention to his connections with Russia's Putin over the past decade! Almost everything that he has done since 2013 is a direct mirror of Hitler's rise to a Fascist Dictatorship from the 1930's to the early 1940's in Europe!

Let me summarize where we are in this situation that compels us to cry out, "Oh, Tyranny"! From the very beginning, (likely 2012 or 2013), we have faced a deliberate effort to destroy every aspect of Democracy in America. America has diligently tried for a decade to ignore the danger despite several authors (as early as 2015) having clearly stated that this was the goal from the beginning. That's a serious charge that we must face!

To make what we've said here so much more real over the past year there have been four instances where someone has used rifles to destroy transformers in power substations. These actions require little knowledge or planning but caused long lasting, power outages in large communities even in the dead of winter. Substations are often in remote locations and are protected only by chain-link fences. They're ideal, easy and effective targets for asymmetric terrorists. Oh, TYRANNY!

Let me try to put everything we have said to date into total perspective. We were pretty much running as a democracy before the advent of a want-to-be dictator who went to Russia to solicit help from a sworn enemy of the United States in 2013! I'm sure that almost everyone in the United States was pretty confident that life here was not all that bad - at least as compared to Russia, North Korea, Saudi Arabia or Hungary. We very much believed in the sanctity of elections, transition of power, the rule of law, the constancy of the constitution and the political independence of our court systems. We believed in our schools and our institutions of higher education - but perhaps more importantly we were assured that we could change our choice if those institutions were perceived to be not to our liking or benefit. Choice is the key to everything. Only when you perceive that there is no choice or that you have had choices taken from you or they have been dictated to you in some unimaginable way that you begin to feel the Angst that your life is on the edge of a very dark abyss indeed.

We have fought many wars with the loss of considerable blood and treasure to ensure and to preserve that freedom of choice as well as this beacon of Democracy. What a shame and a tragic loss for all of those 240 years of hard-fought for good life just to be taken away from us by a domestic cancer that everyone should have recognized almost a decade ago but when once recognized was not taken down with the known actions used to kill it! Such a dangerous cancer should have been destroyed very swiftly at least six years ago. This cancer is the kind that lurks in the minds of weak, lazy, ignorant, but, unfortunately, very greedy, and ambitious people lusting for power. Their lives are driven by a need to greatly compensate for, by artificial means, their tremendous lack of knowledge, competency, personality, compassion, purpose of good for others or of any actual self-worth. They are very pathetic!

132   UNDERSTANDING: Hey, Y'all, we have been watching this horror show for essentially a decade now! How long does it take to get it through your heads that something terribly wrong has been going on here in America for at least ten years? Why have you not all been deafened by the constant and predictably rhetorical nerve shattering DIN that you have been assaulted with from primarily one person for those many years? I've known many con men and persuasive talkers in my lifetime. In every case that I knew personally there was always a very predictable fact. People that came under their influence were completely enamored with them and their "tremendous" capabilities for the good of the cause for two months. They would brag about them and extoll their greatness to all that would listen for about that long. Shortly after that love period they would suddenly - almost abruptly - change their view to one of total avoidance and abhorrence! After that, they would have absolutely nothing good to say about them. Instead, they would seek people out to warn them of the distinct danger of them becoming detrimentally enamored by their evil powers and influences! Why not now? Why not this time?

I admit that in 2016 I must have been very naive. Based upon my experience, I "just knew" that this two-month phenomenon would happen to this imposter that had just been elected. If the two-month rule didn't get him, something more powerful would chew him up and spit him out; if not in real time it would do it over a very long, slow, drawn-out process. That was the very slow but finely grinding millstones of the Federal Government. What I had apparently not counted upon was the tenacity (or total stupidity) of his followers. They clung to him through thick and thin and through disasters, failings, and losing episodes one after another. Oh well, I thought the members of the GOP party who had been in the government for years and who knew the ropes about how to deal with total flakes and charlatans would know how to take him down a peg or two and make it clear he had to toe the line or disappear.

Unfortunately for America, even his harshest critics that
ran against him in the primaries and knew about his cheating,
conning, lying and non-paying and accurately called him out
on all of those gross faults; suddenly fell in line with, swore by
and fervently supported him just like the sycophants of King
Louis XIV's court in 1661 France. Go figure!

So, is history a lesson that we are taught but is often ignored
because "It just is not relevant to our time?" How many of you
lived during the Second World War? A few of you, I would
guess. Have you not seen movies about the Second World
War? Are there any recent TV shows about life and the
resistance movements in France, Poland, the Scandinavian
countries and, yes, even in Germany itself? Many of these are
very graphic, telling and down-right scary. I was very young
when I lived in a place during the Second World War. Even
though I lived safely in America, the whole experience was not
just very inconvenient - it was damn scary. Sugar and other
necessary commodities like gasoline were severely rationed.
There were constant food shortages. We were fortunate to live
on a lot large enough to be able to grow a "victory garden" in
order to be able to get something to eat. We inevitably got
used to that, but that was not the worst part. It was the air
raids that happened almost every night. We had to pull all of
the shades, turn off all outside lights and dim internal lighting
to a minimum and maintain that condition for hours.

History has not only shown us but taught us a great deal
about what went wrong that allowed Hitler and a Fascist
Authoritarian Dictatorship to grow and thrive in Germany.
These history lessons must be taken to heart immediately to
try to stop this wild madness run to becoming a (FAD) here in
the United States. I must warn you that we are about 80% of
the way there now because the Justice Department completely
dropped the ball for two years and did absolutely nothing to
stop the effects of a Treasonous Insurrection after 1/6/21.

134   1: It's now too late to learn from any history lesson that you were ignoring while you were texting love notes to your girlfriend. 2: You have all lived too long enjoying the immense pleasures and freedoms afforded you by the DEMOCRACY of these United States. You take it for granted! 3: By not dropping the punishment bomb early in 2021 we have allowed a very fast growing CANCER that could have been killed in its infancy to metastasize throughout our nation and grow lots of deadly tentacles into the very fabric of our civilization with propaganda, thousands of deliberate lies, race and culture wars and in essence doing everything that was done in Germany (as well as every other Fascist takeover) including banning of books (book burnings in Nazi Germany) control of school boards, curriculum, and what may be taught and what may not be taught. Censorship of speech, written word, the arts, and personal freedoms are right at the top of every list. This list is now much longer than mentioned here, but hopefully you are finally getting the message that this Nation is right now in very dire straits and so near to a final transition to a FASCIST AUTOCRATIC STATE that only very drastic measures can now stop its deadly progress.

So, does anyone now know - just a show of hands - does everyone know that if you do just one wrong move at the ballot box that every pleasure, every right, every joy, every thought, every happy day, every celebration of life, every joyous XMAS, every Happy Birthday that you've known in life will be gone FOREVER? Forever is an extremely long time and in fact is not reversible. The answer is that you must never vote for any Republican in this decade in order to save not just yourself but all of America. Only then are you truly patriots just like your sons, daughters and parents who gave their lives to defend and to keep our civilization alive. Don't laugh! This is deadly serious. We are that close to destruction that drastic measures are required. We only have this one last chance. Don't squander it.

KNOWLEDGE: In the early days of his reign the media
and we could only guess about their intentions and goals for destruction. He did a fair job of pretending to be the Resident. Now they are all telling you to your face exactly what and how they intend to destroy this democracy and replace it entirely with a FASCIST AUTHORITARIAN DICTATORSHIP (FAD). Look at the rash of Fascist laws that have been passed in the "Woke goes to die State." They have been widely publicized and touted to be the supreme achievements of a totally Fascist Governor in his bid to take his Fascism on the road Nationally. He seems intent upon taking away every right and pleasure of everyone that lives in his State.

Did any of you see what most of the speakers said at the 2023 CPAC conference in St. Georges county, Maryland? It was pretty much in your face about the ex-president's plan to take over the GOP and the Nation in his own image and with a variety of Fascist Authoritarian Dictatorships. There is no longer a fog or a curtain concealing their sinister intentions for America. It also was not possible to conceal the reason for the timing of his first campaign rally in Waco, TX on the 30th anniversary of the tragedy at that site. What used to be concealed and could only be guessed at is now in your face with every tweet, pronouncement, event, rally and document. Now that possible indictments may be imminent his screeches are getting more and more shrill and desperate-sounding. Some seem to be so over-the-top that if he were the CEO of a normal company, he would suddenly find his desk and belongings out in the street, and perhaps would be arrested for intimidation of a court officer. So, why does it not seem to apply to the actions of an ex-president? That is the question!

After observing the frenzy of the attendees at CPAC, just what is the appeal for these idiots? Is it being a Bully or a Strong Man? Being Macho? Trying to look tough, decisive or committed? It's a mystery why they follow a pied piper to die!

136 My GOD, GOP! Are you completely blinded by this aura? Is it not merely an illusion with its intended dazzlement (a kind of ancient Greek siren) strategically placed to lure you all to your fate and eventually to your total destruction? What if the other side said these kinds of things to you? What would your reaction be? Would you not be disgusted, horrified or angry? What if your side (as predicted) ends up doing what they are promising to do to others and they end up doing it to you as well? What then? Must I remind every one of you "There can be but only one Dictator", and none of you will be that Dictator. Therefore, by your subservience and your raucous clamoring of support for this FALSE IDOL to which you have cleaved yourselves, you are sealing your very own fates - not to mention that of the entire once free democratic world.

PEOPLE UNDER CONTROL: What is the deadly appeal to follow these FALSE IDOLs (these pied pipers) to their deaths and total destruction? Is it a sense of belonging? Is it a need to have someone that you "trust" to follow? Is it an appeal to those little niggling doubts about yourselves and the resultant feelings of having been forgotten, slighted or cheated by someone? Does it appeal to that cadre of grievances that you have been harboring that are not necessarily related to the ones stated by the false prophet? Does his appearance of fighting for his injustices appeal to your desire to finally have someone that seems willing to fight for your own injustices? Does he seem to be empathetic to your own causes - as a false idol would have been to sooth the Israelites? Does he make it seem like he is constantly a victim of wrong doers but is the glorious warrior that will constantly keep up the fight and will be the one to keep the fight to defend you and your grievances? BS! He's the one with the jet, the magnificent homes and golf courses, the golden toilets and hundreds of key politicians in his pockets! You have none of those things; nor will you ever have anything like that if you follow this Trojan Horse IDOL to the depths of HELL itself!

The first clue is total loyalty! When representatives of the 137 people take an oath of office to serve, they take that oath to support and to defend the Constitution against all enemies both foreign and DOMESTIC! For the president: "I will to the best of my ability, preserve and defend the Constitution of the United States." They don't take a loyalty oath to a person or a party. That is not just a clue that stands out like a red flag or a blaring siren but is something that is executable under section 3 of the 14th amendment of the Constitution. By that section 3, at least 100 of the members of Congress, are not able to serve in Congress, nor is the former Resident of the White House able to run for ANY office of the Federal Government nor of any State. His presence at rallies as a declared candidate is clearly in violation of section 3 of the 14th amendment of the Constitution, and that section should be strictly enforced!

Looking further into the nature of loyalty oaths, we are struck by those rituals that may be associated with gangsters, mobsters, the Cosa Nostra or those organizations simply referred to as the Mafia. These organizations obviously require loyalty oaths to their leaders but they might often go one step further by requiring an act required to prove once and for all your fervor that proves your pledge to take the oath. In order to belong to a Secret Society, you might have to show that you are even more brutal, evil or cruel than the leader himself. You may have to "eliminate" either a close friend, loved one, or perhaps just a total stranger at random as proof of your loyalty. Perhaps that no longer is the case, but the possible existence of that tends to demonstrate the point of how deadly serious the taking of an oath to support one person or an organization of influence could be. It is very much an inwardly focused act, an act of singular preservation, rather than a benevolent, altruistic act directed to the greater good and preservation of everyone else. Haven't we seen enough Al Capone movies to recognize what is going on here? This kind of rhetoric is getting very tiresome indeed and must end now!

138   There's a very distinctive trait that stands out among the terrorist groups that deserves our close attention. One of their processes is to destroy the trust and faith in our principals, traditions and institutions. They tend to ignore every law or legal act that has been legitimately brought against them or requested of them.   It is a means to normalize the total disrespect for and destruction of the rule of law.   This is something that they do very predictably and is done without any thought process or hesitation. It is part of the mantra that they have bought into with constant indoctrination. However, (and this is the essential element that makes this kind of Asymmetric Warfare so effective) they know that law-abiding citizens who want to preserve their democratic way of life would never do anything like this. Thus, a kind of mental quandary is set up in the minds of the law-abiding citizens as to why any reasonable person would ever consider doing anything like this. That purposeful confusion is the smoke screen that delays very necessary and appropriate action from law-abiding citizens to take immediate action to stop that form of lawlessness. It makes the real patriots essentially come to the street fight with soup spoons rather than knives, brass knuckles or bludgeons. Figuratively speaking of course.

Like robins who get drunk feeding on Pyracantha berries, the scene often ends in a feeding frenzy and ends with drunk birds rolling on the ground. That seems to be the pattern of those that get caught up in the propaganda frenzy from a campaign rally that's like a "revivalist" event. It's not politically correct, but there seems to be a strong resemblance to huge rallies in parts of Europe in the late '30s or early '40s. What happens in a frenzy is a strong desire to outdo the person next to you in your outward appearance of being "more patriotic" than the next person. It's absolutely a characteristic of mob rule as we experienced on 1/6/21 at the ellipse, or more destructively at the Capitol building for three plus hours. Mob dynamics is not a support for freedom or democracy!

The asymmetry of TIME is perhaps one of the most sinister weapons of the MAGA GOP war on our democracy. It is the most basic element of an Asymmetric Warfare that can be used to destroy any nation. Let me explain: Terrorists can plan in secret over very long periods of time to do something very destructive. There are no rules that they are bound to abide by regarding the transparency of their actions. Therefore, they can break any rule or law in an instant and have very detrimental results immediately that cannot be dealt with in real time because our court system is so inefficient that it takes months to years to finally take action against a subversive or terrorist act. Witness how long it has taken for Fani Willis to even come close to putting together an indictment for attempts to overturn the 2020 election. It's been more than 2 years since 1/6/21 and there are still no indictments of anyone at the top who planned and executed that riot. In effect, Terrorists can do real damage immediately and can live, plan and execute over and over again for years while the justice system is still just thinking about it. Immediate feedback and action is crucial to stop terrorism.

That's why we've said from the beginning that when your nation is being threatened by a Terrorist group that is determined to destroy your democracy and replace it with a Fascist Authoritarian Dictatorship (FAD), immediate action to stop it as soon as possible is paramount to killing the Cancer before it can metastasize and destroy your Nation. Long-term jail sentences are about all that terrorists understand. They must be swift, immediate and consequential. Short of that, there are much less effective methods that should have been applied from the start. At the very least, those who are in charge of protecting the democracy of the Nation should have been meeting and gaming the Terrorists' options from day one. Then they might have been able to anticipate their next steps in time to take decisive and effective measures to "cut them off at the pass", as in days of old!

140 A way to mitigate attempts to overthrow a democracy, when all else seems to fail, is to stage huge demonstrations throughout the country. This seems to work better in small compact countries than in huge expansive ones like America. It is very difficult to organize effective marches in so many diverse regions of a very large country. The worst part is that individual states are trying to pass laws that would prohibit the "free speech" of peaceful demonstrations. Even though they can be organized almost immediately they don't seem to produce much more than a "hill of beans" here in America.

DWINDLING OPTIONS: Why doesn't the government run more like a business? When a president of a company lies he is likely to find his desk and all of his belongings out in the street and may also be handed a warrant for his arrest for committing a crime either against the company or in the name of the company. When a person is being vetted for a job as president of a company, I can guarantee you that that person's character, behaviors, employee histories and community records are thoroughly reviewed before he even gets near an interview. So why are we so shoddy in any similar process for the position of the most important person in the world? It is clear that we have ended up in both the House and Senate with people that are absolutely unqualified for those jobs. Normally in business, they would be fired or forced to resign because they are totally incompetent to do the job that they were hired to do. A case in point is a Representative from a district near NYC that has lied about his entire resume. If he worked for a company he would not have even gotten the job, much less be in it and manage to stay in it, under these entirely false premises.

What does a population do when there seem to be no more options to turn around or to kill an insurrection hell-bent upon destroying a democracy? When the effectiveness of voting has been nullified and the laws have been set against your being able to use normal democratic means to fix a situation that clearly has the nation headed for a "FAD", what do you do? The survival of democracy is so far-reaching, and of an importance that it is orders of magnitude above any other consideration, that it would seem that very extraordinary measures or procedures must be brought to bear to resolve the issue favorably for democracy. There can be no other conclusion than this. Does that mean martial law must be imposed until the situation has been mitigated to the point that normalcy can be restored? I assure you that this is not an uncommon situation; It's been done many times before. Sometimes there are military coups, but that is generally when the direction is more toward autocracy than democracy.

Sometimes, one just has to take a second to amend a totally dire situation for the better interests and the survival of the democracy in the shortest possible time. During WWII there were resistance movements in Poland, the Scandinavian countries, France and, oh, yes, even in Germany itself. The people realized that every normal option that had been available to them had been methodically and systematically eliminated. Their ability to resolve their dire situations with the former democratic ways had been completely taken away.

When you compare the survival of a democracy of 300 million people to the killing of even as many as 30 children in a classroom there can be no conclusion other than that the former is orders of magnitude more important than the latter. And yet, very sudden measures are always required to resolve the school situation as quickly as possible. Is it even a reasonable proposition that we try to use extremely slow legal processes and court procedures, requiring years to conclude, to try to eliminate a Terrorist cancer from the United States as soon as possible? Does this even make any sense? Just think about that for a very long moment if you will, please. This is a concern that will give your heart a very great pause.

142 HORRIFIC STATUS OF AMERICA TODAY: So much of what was predicted weeks and days ago in this book has not only come to pass but has shocked our nation and the entire world. It is so Fascist in nature that it must be shared with the world before this edition goes to press! It is proof of how far America' democracy has been corrupted.

A judge in Amarillo, Texas Ruled on a case over which he had absolutely no jurisdiction. The case was "judge-shopped" to his court by a group of people that had absolutely no standing- in his court either. This case should have been thrown out immediately based on the grounds that the plaintiffs had no standing. The tort was frivolous and totally without merit. He ruled that a drug was improperly approved for use 23 years ago by the ONLY United States government agency (FDA) that is tasked with the responsibility of protecting the public with labs and scientific data to verify the safety and validity of all of our drugs. Fourty eight months were used to approve the drug - far more than more commonly used drugs. It's been used by millions of women for 20 years with an exceedingly high safety record. Also, the drug had been used safely in Europe for 13 years before its approval in the United States.

No judge has jurisdiction over the only agency in America that is authorized to protect the public against unsafe drugs or drugs with dubious utility or merit. His ruling was clearly biased and spoke of things that are totally irrelevant to the function of drug testing and public safety. This was clearly a MAGA inspired end run around our institutions and democratic way of life. Clearly it is a part of a plan to destroy the validity of our sustaining and protective institutions. A democracy cannot tolerate one person with no knowledge or expertise taking the rule of law and our freedoms away from us. That is a Fascist Dictatorship and it should be immediately recognized as such by everyone. This further proves my earlier point that we have let all of this go on far too long.

Another extremely disturbing thing happened this week that may not have happened if everyone had been arrested, tried and jailed in the two years following the insurrection. Now it is clear that we failed to do what was absolutely necessary when we could. There was an AR-15 shooting in a Protestant school in Nashville, TN that killed three nine year olds and three adults before the gunman was shot and killed. This past week school children from throughout the region marched on the capitol to demand legislative action to reduce gun violence and destruction from mass shootings. "We need to know that the children that we left alive at school in the morning will be alive when we go to pick them up at night."

The Tennessee legislature has a supermajority in both houses as the result of extremely biased gerrymandering of the state voting districts. When the student demonstration started in the gallery of the house chamber, three democratic congressmen went to the "well of the House" to join in the demonstration that was chanting from the chamber gallery. Two were newly installed black freshmen and one was a Caucasian woman representative. A bullhorn was used to enhance the sound of their chants. As a result, the Republican dominated legislature voted to expel the three from being members of the house. The two blacks were expelled but the Caucasian woman was spared the action. The three each gave a twenty-minute talk before the vote to plead their case. Over and over they made the point about how this legislature eagerly voted to ban books and Drag queen shows but not to vote to do anything about the increasing number of murdered children in the schools in the state - murdered by AR-15 type of weapons. They added that dead children were not able to read any books or to see Drag Queen shows!

It was very clear that this legislature had a MAGA GOP based philosophy and mind set. The voting out of two blacks at the exclusion of one Caucasian woman was very suggestive that 144 they were also of a white supremacist frame of mind as well! The news media pointed out many times that the KKK was started in Tennessee in 1865. There also seemed to be a connection with the later Jim Crow laws of some of the southern states. The whole event instantly made the "Tennessee Three", world famous, and gave a huge boost in their quest for civil rights and the re-establishment of Democracy for all. The event also clearly demonstrated to the world the total hypocrisy of the present MAGA GOP movement as well as its members. They were not at all ashamed to have their Fascist Autocratic ideas displayed openly for everyone in the world to see. Remember my words in chapter 14, "That is total commitment! As a result, you cannot shame them, embarrass them, guilt them, humiliate them or even try to negotiate with them, because they will not be shaken from their oath or their cause."

These two total anomalies and stark contradictions to the norms of a democracy suddenly showed the entire world how dangerously close to a Fascist Authoritarian Dictatorship we have become in so few years. The fact that these two brazen events happened within weeks of each other only underscores how close to the end we have come because we failed to take immediate action to kill this deadly cancer when it was first detected (if not in 2013 - 2016) when its ugly venomous head was completely exposed in full view to the world on 1/6/21.

There can never be any excuse for inaction or unnecessary delay when it comes to killing this kind of cancer that can rapidly devour a democracy. Every minute of delay only allows it to grow exponentially, plan a thousand next steps, and to recruit new warriors while growing deadly tentacles into every inch of the fabric of our democratic society. Very rapidly those tentacles become like the roots of old, well established trees - they cannot be cut or "rooted out" even if the upper part of the tree is diminished or cut down. Not even new laws or leaders will be able to reverse the extensive 145 damage that has been permanently caused by their rapid growth. Have you ever seen what even an insignificant weed can do to a concrete sidewalk or driveway if that weed is inclined to grow up through that almost formidable barricade? Have you ever seen what happens to that same driveway or the foundation of your house when the root of a nearby tree grows in size under it? It can totally destroy that foundation and it is almost impossible to remove or to kill that root!

So, from just these last events, we seem to be so much further down the path to destruction that even if we vote the right party into the Presidency, House and Senate, we may still not be able to save our democracy without far more drastic procedures. I can only think of what it took to rid Germany of its Fascist Authoritarian Dictatorship. It was not at all simple and it required the loss of thousands of lives and significant outside intervention from Nations from the free world.

We just had another mass shooting in a bank in Louisville KY. Five are dead including the shooter and there are 8 injured. When will this insanity stop? Many MAGA GOP governors are passing laws that make the acquisition of deadly weapons (that are only intended for wartime use) available to younger buyers without including licenses, measures for training, background checks, or mental competency. They also allow open or concealed carry. The police response was within three minutes and "perhaps prevented further deaths". How many times have we heard this meaningless phrase as well as "our thoughts and prayers are with the survivors"? There shouldn't have been any lives lost and "thoughts and prayers" do absolutely nothing to keep even one person from being killed by a gun that should never ever be allowed in the hands of a single citizen that is not at that moment serving in a war. The bullets from this gun leave the muzzle at 3,000 ft. per second! That is 2,045 miles per hour!! For a child in a school 146   room or a customer in a bank, they are going to be dead before they hear the sound from the first shot. Three minutes is an eternity when a shooter can fire one shot per second. That could be 180 shots in those three minutes that it took to get the police to the scene. Even a guard in a school would take minutes to get to an active shooter in the building. The only thing that can stop this carnage is to eliminate the availability of this weapon from the public in the first place.

Again, how does the shooting of even 5 people in this one event (out of 145 events in just the first three months of this year) compare to the loss of 300 million lives of Americans if we are taken over by a Fascist Authoritarian Dictatorship? Think very long and hard about that comparison. Every one of you 300 million citizens, stop and think of the total ruination of your lives and that of your families if just one particular person wins the election in 2024. Please, everyone, read up about the lives of the people in Germany (and Europe) prior to and during WWII. Just one movie is all that it would take for you to be convinced that there is no way that you would ever want to live in that situation. There's at least one way to end it; never vote for the GOP in the next decade. On the other hand, what is it that is done immediately to end the threat when there is an active shooter in a school or a bank?

This is a very serious business. Perhaps it is time for parts of America to make some very serious decisions! There is so much that is "bad headed" that just cannot be corrected with elections! The MAGA GOP, in way too many States, are acting like they know that elections in their States will not have any effect on the makeup of the government, the legislative bodies, the courts or their supreme court! Fascism, Authoritarianism and being Ruled by a Dictator is the name for that kind of Government. By then, Democracy is a long way back in the rearview mirror - fading away fast, never to be seen again!

ISSUES, NOT SOLUTIONS: Obfuscation - the action of making something obscure, unclear, or unintelligible. Using it in a sentence you might say; "when confronted with sharp questions they resort to obfuscation".

Why do I bring this word up now? Actually there is a very good reason! The short paragraph above gives you the clue to figure out what comes next. Even after four years in office, two years since and the two campaign years before, the news media is still trying to figure out why the entire MAGA GOP seems to have gone completely bonkers. You'd think that after a decade of his hyperbole, lies and total hypocrisy they would have figured it out! Come on, folks, a decade is a very long time to recognize the character of a charlatan, grifter, con man; and a would be Fascist Autocratic Dictator.

When you are operating within a "democratic" base, but your goals from day one are the total destruction of a democracy, you must start from the beginning to appear that you are a valid part of the democratic process. Important principles, norms, institutions, traditions, structures, laws and agencies must be gradually destroyed and normalized as being either corrupt or completely unreliable. That's why almost everything they talk about are ISSUES rather than SOLUTIONS. Guess what, issues can almost always be blamed on the opposition which directs the attention away from the fact that they are not actually doing any good for the cause. If they start talking about solutions, then citizens begin to expect to have positive results coming from their party. When there are none they are in the soup for lack of performance. It's the oldest trick in the book. Before the election they talk about law and order and inflation. After winning the election they talk about cultural issues and "wokeness". The media asks why aren't you working on inflation? Do you think that we are crazy? That just gets us into trouble because we won't have any results there!

148   TRUST in everything must be destroyed: but you can't do it with a sledgehammer! There is no faster way of destroying TRUST than lying all of the time! However, when you lie all of the time it is implied that your opposition must also be doing the same. That also destroys trust in the integrity of the democracy minded opposition; even between themselves. That is why even when there is a video of a MAGA GOP stating very clearly he would never in a lifetime do a certain thing but a year later he is doing what he stated that he would never do; he can't be shamed or embarrassed about the contradiction. It was a lie a year ago and it is a different lie a year later! So what? Everyone lies, don't they? Gotcha! You were thinking like a normal law abiding citizen with morals and scruples. It's all part of the plan. There is no better way to keep the law abiding citizens off guard than to completely boggle their minds about behavior that they just cannot fathom. You should have read <u>We Must Think like Putin or have Voting Booths in Moscow</u>. Moswee M Peach, 2019.

So, why does the media keep wondering, when the MAGA GOP did so badly in the 2022 midterms, why they are still doubling down and doing even more crazy bats–t? Again, you have to understand 240 years of democracy has been reassuring, not very stressful, and totally disarming. We have had decades of relying upon the stability of our institutions, laws, constitution, voting and of those who administer our voting processes. We have had a strong belief that people, including politicians, are basically honest and moral. And, perhaps more importantly, we haven't been challenged by a threatening war for seven or eight decades - essentially for three generations. Unlike the Ukrainians who have been fighting a war of survival with Putin for almost a decade, we are not desperately fighting for life or death outcomes - at

least not yet. It is very hard to awaken a sleeping giant that has been lulled into a sense of total security by three generations of peace and prosperity. It's two years past time to get fired up
and to fight like hell! Excusing the news media for their   149 lack of knowledge about history to see what has been going on for almost a decade, we must get a grip, see the big picture and resolve to fight like hell to save this democracy, we must beat back the roaring flames of a determined (FAD) Fascist Authoritarian Dictatorship. The media didn't properly warn this nation of the dire consequences that are essentially upon us right now. We are dearly paying the price for a lack of foresight even though many books were written to adequately warn us all about this years ago.

Even if we are at all successful, now, it may take a decade to fully recover because of how extensive the damage has been allowed to penetrate into our national roots! The fact that the DOJ failed to go after the top-tier perpetrators almost immediately is a fact that we will greatly regret for an eternity. That total dereliction of duties for two years, was criminal for the enormous irreversible damage that was able to grow and metastasize throughout our society. There can be absolutely no forgiveness for this neglectfully criminal behavior. Never!

Why is it that even after at least six years of the most flagrant violations of almost every norm of our formerly well running democracy, we seem totally incapable of getting a grip upon how dangerous it is to allow any of these MAGA GOP terrorists anywhere near our government? This is especially true of the ring leader who "is currently running" for President. There is more than enough evidence of his acts of treason that the 14th amendment must keep him away from our politics for the rest of his life! There can be no other option and that goes for the rest of his co-conspirators in the Congress or any other part of our government. Above all else, there is the most important consideration. It took 240 years to build this marvelous experiment in government and it is a moral imperative that it must not be allowed to be destroyed by a Fascist group!

150   ACCOUNTABLE or INVINCIBILE: Are humans basically animals except that they have RULES and LAWS? Animals in general live by their wits and need to be predatory to survive. Their instincts are to find prey, stalk it, catch it and kill it, if possible, in order to have something to feed themselves and their families. So what is society? Society, apparently, is the condition where humans have discovered over millennia that by growing food and raising their meat proteins that they are able to live in close proximity to each other by agreeing to and following a system of rules and laws that keeps their animal instincts on a tight leash. Societies tend to be characterized by shared values, beliefs and cultures. These are often distilled into that set of rules that both allows them freedom of choice and living styles without those choices unduly impinging upon their neighbors or upon the society itself.

The keys to everything are the rules and laws and a belief in them to the extent that they will be agreeably followed in order to be able to maintain the advantages of living in that society. Penalties, and punishments, however, must be made very clear in order to correct for those aberrations in behavior that will come to play from time to time. By now It should be abundantly clear that no society can survive without both the laws and the punishments for aberrant behaviors. If either of these are removed or ignored, the result will be a rapid decay leading to changes that are abhorrent to the society itself. That is primarily why both the Constitution and the Rule of Law are so important to the survival of the functioning democracy of the United States. Actually, this corollary is key to the survival of every society or nation - even for the most primitive of tribes. Just as you may have just had an "Aha!" moment you are perhaps suddenly seeing the direction of this discussion.

OK, let's do it! Fact1: a society or nation cannot exist without laws or punishments. Fact 2: A society or nation where a large percentage of people ignore rules or laws is doomed and bound to rapidly fail. Why is this so relevant to us now?

What would happen if a part of your town suddenly sank into a deep sinkhole and those people suddenly found themselves in an entirely different world filled with prehistoric, predatory animals like the dinosaurs. Suddenly, their focus would change from just "getting along to git along" to that of a desperate game of survival. Now, every morsel of food is a game of wits and drastic competition. There's no helping your neighbor, no sharing, no cooperation or congeniality. It's every man for himself and the crueler the better. It literally is a race to the bottom - every pun intended. You spy on your neighbor to try to catch him at a moment when he has just found a morsel to eat so that you can swoop in and take it from him - by deadly force if necessary. All rules are gone and there are no punishments for being meaner than your neighbor. To survive, you must be more cunning, more aggressive, more of a bastard than your competition to survive. When the rules and laws are gone and you are vying to be the winner - the king of the hill - it is an all-out "Go for Broke" competition.

If people feel that they are invincible and that there can be no consequences, they will do the most despicable, cruel, absurd things to other people and be absolutely proud of it. There are even secret groups on the internet where the goal is to plan and stage a mass shooting. You get the best score for killing the most innocent people - especially if they are young unprotected children! Consequences? To play, you just have to expect to be killed as the result of the successful execution. Therefore, since that is your stance going in, you are not going to be swayed by any laws, rules or punishments. They are of no consequence to your decision to proceed. You are able to do the most heinous of crimes without any deterrent or feeling of any consequences that may have meaning for you. Organized crime has that same kind of mantra and it is often used as a test of your commitment and loyalty to the crime boss.

152 So, what is the difference between the methods of Organized crime and those of the MAGA GOP? Essentially, absolutely nothing. The members of organized crime know that they are so ruthless, that it is unlikely that any law enforcement will be able to touch them. They reduce the likelihood of being caught by brutally eliminating any of their members or family members who dare to "rat on the gang" or give evidence to the police. That execution is most likely done in a way that all other members of either their gang or of a competing gang will be dramatically made aware of how brutal and horrific that execution was accomplished. It is also a serious warning lesson for those in law enforcement as well.

So what about the MAGA GOP? Some of what happens in a gang happens within the ranks of that party, albeit to a much lesser degree. In general, we do not see politicians being "rubbed out". However, they have likely been forced to take an oath and a pledge of loyalty to the leader - which they have been made to feel that they must obey. There are also serious political or career consequences if they fall out of line. They are definitely made aware of the damage that will come to their future if they falter. That is why we see so many of them vote on bills in the most illogical way. It just drives the media absolutely bonkers! Their minds just cannot wrap around that kind of behavior. Ok, so maybe that isn't everything.

In a democracy, there is the public to worry about. There is the vote that can eliminate their job. You see, there are two ways that they can suddenly lose their cushy jobs. So, it is always a gamble as to which dangerous force that they fear most. However, if they feel that neither votes or demonstrations will be effective in taking away their power, they have absolutely no fear to vote the party line, the bosses line, or the line of the party leader. One more, huge aspect to this new fact. If they no longer fear the vote they can double down and vote for the most insane unpopular laws and just not give a D–N!

Guess what just happened? You have just witnessed the unveiling of the MAGA GOP party as being synonymous to a crime syndicate that is operating on a national scale. This revelation explains a plethora of puzzlements that have plagued the media and the American voters for almost a decade. More importantly, that depiction effectively sorts out the mysteries of why the MAGA GOP consistently votes for ridiculous punitive laws and procedures that run counter to the needs or wishes of the American public. That is because, as a syndicate, they feel that they are totally immune from reprisals, legal action, lawsuits, being voted out of power, or removed by legislative or governmental actions. Like a syndicate, they have assured themselves that they are already totally free from harassment. And, like a syndicate, they are controlled by a strong man at the top who calls all of the shots, and directs all of their moves. It basically is operating like a national crime syndicate.

The minions that support the boss are sycophants that are not just under his spell, but have pledged their very soul to being his "enforcers". They have taken the oath to defend the "boss" at all costs. Just look at the minions that are already serving time in jail for things that they did only because they were obeying orders. Take note that instead of turning witness against the boss in order to save themselves, they took the hit for the person who required them to do the thing that landed them in prison. Does that remind anyone of being like a crime syndicate? Yes, I thought so!

So, why didn't the DOJ go after the syndicate as soon as possible after it made its intentions so dramatically clear on

1/6/21? Were there threats of syndicate style reprisals? Was it made clear that lives would be at stake if legal actions were taken? Come to think of it, there has been nothing but that kind of threat being made in abundance after the indictments in Manhattan, NY.

154   It is beginning to become all so clear. The patterns are beginning to fall into place. There are threats being made against the prosecutor as well as members of his family. There are threats against the judge and members of his family. There are threats of violence that will erupt throughout the entire United States if these and other expected indictments are forthcoming. The media has been puzzled as to why a sane man would resort to such crass, 'ineffective" behaviors.

However, it all becomes so clear if they are dealing with a mob boss. They are essentially dealing with a mob boss and it now apparently involves one hundred plus members of the House of Representatives, about forty members of the Senate and God knows how many members of the Supreme Court. They have weaponized a dozen key committees of the House to take on the task of running congressional interference in all of these expected court indictments "on an official government business basis". Some of these committees have been tasked with the role of "officially" harassing the prime opposition candidates before the upcoming 2024 election. Of course, all of these plans were made years ago through a series of meetings as well as other guarded conversations. What in hell has the Democratic party been doing all this time? Counting on normal voting to end this well-orchestrated madness? Are you kidding me? Did any vote ever take out Al Capone? No, I don't think so! Did any vote ever eliminate the head of the SS? No, I think not. It took the death of hundreds of thousands of brave young men and women and many free nations to end that madness.

It sounds like we need to start dealing in terms of the RICO statute. It is way past time to be pretending that this nation is dealing with a normal candidate that is just running for office. It is time to recognized the vast mounds of horrific evidence that clearly defines the real threat - THE TOTAL THREAT to the continued existence of our democracy. Do it NOW – TODAY!!

DIRE CONSEQUENCES that are IMMINENT   155

Let me try to give you a feel of how bad things have gotten, but more importantly, how bad it will get if one National Crime Syndicate, Crime Boss, is elected to be Resident in 2024. There is so much that has happened in even in the past six months. There is far more that is happening daily in towns and cities, across the nation, directed to alter control of school districts and public libraries with right wing ideologues. None of these can be altered simply by elections or the courts. This applies to Berlin style Book burning in schools and libraries.

First, it is so bad that even if a Democrat is elected to be President, and has a majority in both the House and Senate, this nation will still be in extreme danger because of the considerable damage that has already been done to our political way of life. This is a direct result of the two-year hiatus of the Justice department under Merrick Garland, to prosecute the most responsible MAGA leaders in 2021. That lack of action may very well cost this Nation its beloved Democracy.

For the second, just stop and think of the worst possible day that you may have in your life. It might be a day that you discovered that you had stage III colon cancer. It might be a day that you learn that your wife or husband has terrible cancer. It might be a day that you were involved in a terrible car crash that maimed you for the rest of your life. It may be the day that your favorite child was slaughtered by an idiot with an AR-15 at school. Whatever it is, multiply that day by

365 and then again by the number of years to the end of your life. Every day of the rest of your life will be like that worst day. Just stop and think about that consequence for a very long time and concentrate on every possible feeling you would be feeling, every day, for the rest of your lives. Now consider this. If one MAGA crime boss is elected in 2024, your life will

156   be as bad, if not worse, than what you just considered, and this will start no more than 5 months after if the MAGA Crime National Syndicate takes over the government in 2024.

You don't believe me? Just listen to what the MAGA syndicate is telling you every day. They have a manifesto to dismantle the Constitution and the Democratic form of government within 5 months of being installed as Resident of the United States. It's called Project 2025 and is freely described on the Trump campaign website.   At the start, it will greatly expand Presidential powers to give him control over most, if not all, of the formerly "independent" agencies of the government. ("Trump and Allies Forge Plans to Increase Presidential Power in 2025", Doug Mill, New York Times, published July 17, 2023 and updated July 18, 2023 by Jonathan Swan, Charlie Savage and Maggie Haberman) Every American citizen must read this manifesto as soon as possible and particularly before the 2024 election. The man is not being coy. He is telling everyone, including Republicans, what your life will be like for the rest of your lives.

I know most of you have not been to Russia, North Korea, Iran, Turkey or now the brave Ukraine. However, I would dare say that you would not want to go live in any of those places at the present time. Why is that? Oh, Tyranny! The Tyranny of it all. Laws have been passed that fine you, jail you, or put you to death just for either doing something you used to do all of your lives or not doing something that the law says you must do. That is not freedom! That's pure hell - and that is what your lives will be like after the 5th month of 2025. And all of you, sycophant MAGA supporters, do you think that you are somehow immune? H-ll no! You are the ones who know too much about how he got back into power. You will be the cannon fodder that is the first to go to prison or be killed. There can be only one dictator and none of you qualify for that. Sorry! I would think about this for a very long time. NOW!

I KNOW that MANY are WONDERING   157

I was very young during the latter part of WWII, but I was aware of horrors that were being perpetrated upon the citizens of Germany as well as the rest of Europe. Since then, I've studied a great deal about the atrocities and the fear that was instilled into the citizenry of that entire continent by Hitler's Fascist Nazi regime. I am aware of many of the ways his rise to power was accomplished within a "Democratic German Republic". I knew people who lived in Berlin and Yugoslavia during the rise of Hitler, Nazism and the terror that prevailed until Europe was liberated by Allied forces in May 1945. The one thing that stands out in everything I have studied is the fact that the number one issue above all else was the gradual way that the takeover was accomplished.

People could feel what was going on and they understood the consequences. But as long as the government, the justice department or the courts either did nothing or were not able to do anything, the people felt helpless to change the deadly course even if they knew that it was imperative to do so. They constantly wished that someone of authority would act to either slow down the progression or stop it all together. A friend told me that she would go to hear the Berlin Philharmonic. All the music that she loved was being played (Mozart, Beethoven, Brahms), but she could not "feel" it or be able to appreciate it. She was numb and devoid of any feelings because of the terrible situations of her surroundings. It was as if she were in a catatonic state. Everyone wondered why the politicians that had been in government for many years did not take the action that they surely knew to take to stop this terrible progression. They worried why they did nothing to alter its course! So much could have been done throughout those early years to end that cancerous growth. However, creeping Fascism must first be recognized, and then dramatic action must be taken to destroy it! It's imperative! NOW!

158   What must be understood is that normal Democratic processes like voting and the courts are no match for a well-planned process to overthrow a government. In the case of Germany and other European countries, resistance movements were used to directly eliminate key figures that held the greatest sway in how successful the Fascist takeover could proceed. Laws and courts were no match to stop the aggressive march to an Authoritarian government. A large part of the basis for a cancerous takeover is the total disregard for laws, courts and elections. When voting no longer matters and courts are months to years too slow to deter cancerous growth, very serious actions absolutely must be taken to avoid total calamity and a total loss of a democracy. Martial law may be just one of the actions needed to counter the threat. Putting perpetrators in jail very early and for very long sentences is an absolute imperative and a very necessary way to end this.

Known key instigators should have had their emails, laptops and computers confiscated on January 7th, 2021. All communications and files needed to be acquired. Perhaps this would not have happened on 1/7/21, but as soon after 1/21/21 as possible. Yes, I know, there would be a large outrage about political persecution. Far better this than alternative of   159 letting the leaders of the National Crime Syndicate run amuck and continue to plan, proselytize supporters and propagate more lies - including the Big Lie! It was clear to the entire world that the MAGA party, headed by its Mob Boss, tried to overthrow a sitting government by force on 1/6/21 and as such committed Insurrection against the United States. All the people that were in the Capitol illegally should have been rounded up in buses and taken to a temporary holding area in a warehouse or school gymnasium. Well, that clearly didn't happen, so we are left with an intangible mess to try to bring justice to tens of thousands of people and their leaders. No wonder there are so many people wondering if those in charge really believe in preserving our Democracy. I really hope so!

What law-abiding citizens have been wondering about for such a long time is why in Hell are we counting on trying to save this democracy with old methods and techniques when the downsides of failure are so permanent? There is no time to sit back, singing Kumbaya, and believing, hope against hope and odds against odds, that somehow by using the vote (that has been so corrupted by now that it is not open for all to use) that Democracy will prevail by chance. My God, man, the odds of any Fascist winning must be an absolute ZERO - no chance! The vote just cannot be counted on! That is what happened to the people of Germany and after it happened, there was absolutely no way to go back to normal without a 4-year WWII and the loss of tens of thousands of lives. Who'd save us?

No, there is no way that any member of the MAGA crime syndicate can be allowed to run for office. By their declared oaths to destroy America they must not only be disqualified to run or serve, but also must be removed from the jobs in which they are already being paid to do. They are simply not qualified, nor are they performing any of the job description requirements. They are slackers, grifters, and glory seekers.

Let me make this very clear to everyone. The MAGA National Crime Syndicate IS NOT A LEGITIMATE POLITICAL PARTY! It is not here to serve the people of the United States in any way shape or form. They have, either directly or by their actions, broken their oaths of office to defend the Constitution and to uphold the rule of law. So, again, decent law-abiding citizens are wondering why any of them are even able to run for office -

especially the Crime Boss who is running for just two very dangerous reasons; 1. to either avoid prosecution or incarceration, or to be pardoned from such actions. 2. to convert our democracy into a Fascist dictatorship in only 5 months after he or a MAGA Crime Syndicate cohort wins the count of the electoral college. Like a school shooting, this is so serious that it CANNOT EVER BE ALLOWED to HAPPEN!

160   That simply means that no one of the MAGA Crime Syndicate can ever run for office and that is especially true of the Syndicate's Crime Boss or any of his close cohorts that were involved in the Treasonous 1/6/21 Armed Insurrection against the United States of America. It also includes close sympathizers who have supported the Big Lie and the 1/6/21 attempt to overtake our government by force with an unruly mob involving tens of thousands of armed MAGA Warriors!

Again, I'm reminded of a play written by Max Frisch in 1958 called The Firebugs. In the play, Gottlieb Biedermann, a successful Swiss businessman, offers his attic for the night to a homeless man as a place to sleep. There have been many fires set recently in the neighborhood, so naturally Gottlieb is fearful that the homeless man might be a firebug. However, as a wealthy businessman it is more important to him to appear to be generous and compassionate than to be fearful. Later the boarder invites a friend into the attic to stay without getting permission from Gottlieb. That upsets Gottlieb, but he is persuaded that it is ok because everyone knows that he is so generous and caring - thus appealing to his ego and a sense of responsibility of being mindful of others who may be less fortunate than himself.

Later, he discovers that the two have brought many barrels of gasoline to the attic and have stored them there. By now, even though he senses the worst of these two, he is now fearful of what they might do if he is not kind, considerate and helpful to them so as to not provoke them into taking the worst possible action that they are now able to take against him. He does everything to appease them by feeding them and finally giving them the matches that they are so eager to obtain. By now, he clearly senses the danger that his house is in but tries to appease them with goodness and kindness to spare his home. You, my friends, can guess the end of this play. This is the parable of the takeover of Germany and Europe by Hitler.

SO, WHY IS THIS so IMPORTANT NOW?   161

If you read the play or a synopsis of it online, you will find many themes that're portrayed. The first is SELF-DECEPTION. The owner of the house wants to believe many things about himself that are just not true. The second is APATHY. Those who are studying these two firebugs intellectually know their danger but are not interested in doing anything about them - like calling the police. The third is NEED for APPROVAL. Gottlieb has such a need for approval that he desperately tries to make friends with the firebugs by laughing at what he takes for jokes when they are telling him what they intend to do to his home. The fourth is GUILT. Gottlieb feels guilty because deep down he senses who these two men are but is more inclined to lie about them than admit what he has sensed to the police - perhaps out of fear for his home. The fifth is MANIPULATION. The firebugs gain acceptance by verbal manipulation and <u>intimidation</u>. One claims to be a wrestler to <u>intimidate</u> Gottlieb with his strength and dominance to keep him from throwing them out of his house.

There are dire things going on right now in the fall of 2023. The MAGA Crime Syndicate Crime Boss is indicted for crimes against the state and election fraud in several locations. He is using various forms of social media to threaten judges, prosecutors, witnesses and possible jurors with slanderous and scurrilous taunts and, in many cases, threats to their families and themselves. In almost every other similar case the indicted would be held in jail until the trial starts many months later. Apparently, because he had been a President of the United States and is again running for that office again, very unusual, lenient considerations have been extended to him to stay out of jail until time for trial. Even though the judges have laid down the law that this behavior must stop or there will be consequences - it has become far worse and more frequent.

162   There can be only one solution, and every parent knows this, every teacher knows this, every judge knows this, every employer knows this, and every citizen of the United States knows this. As painful as it may seem and even as the consequences might be too great, the authority that is being taunted and tested by belligerent behavior must act swiftly to stop this kind of dangerous behavior immediately. The perpetrator must be put in jail immediately, and communication privileges curtailed even despite the threats of violence or further intimidation by others who may be sympathetic to his/her cause. There cannot be any more 'Herr Gottlieb' behaviors to try to appease or ameliorate this dangerous, destructive behavior. Many said that since it's been years later that we should overlook the dangerous, treasonous attempt to overthrow the government on 1/621. No, there can NEVER be forgiveness for such a heinous, despicable, self-serving crime against all of humanity.

Such willfully dangerous people, such as the suspected firebugs in the attic with many barrels of gasoline or a Stump follower with an AR-15 in a school, should not be allowed to follow through with their sinister plots to either burn down the house or to slaughter children. These things are far more important than even law and order can handle. Even at extreme risk and peril they must not be allowed to happen. EVER! The same goes for a person or a National Crime Syndicate or a Crime Boss destroying the Democracy of the United States. Once the danger has been identified - and it clearly has been fully identified - nothing can be either allowed to change or the outcome of a lottery like an election with crooked referees. EVERYTHING leading to even the slightest possibility must be fully eliminated before any election. Those people all must be banned from ever running for office or substantial position for the rest of their lives! To do anything otherwise is pure insanity and spells certain death. You would never allow the storage of gasoline in your attic, WOULD you?

YES, THERE REALLY is a POINT and a CONCLUSION   163

Why is it not the headlines of every newspaper and news outlet every day that MAGA is not, nor have they ever been, a legitimate political party. All MAGA is a National (or an International) Crime Syndicate! If it wasn't clear to everyone before, it has certainly been made very clear by the RICO charges brought by Fani Willis and the Fulton County Grand Jury indictments against Donald Trump and 18 of his Crime Syndicate cohorts on August 14, 2023. This is a fact that just cannot be ignored any longer. This is a fact that is deadly, dangerous and extremely serious to the survival of the USA!

If there was a way to stop one MAGA AR-15 swaggering crazy person from gaining entry to a school ready to massacre two dozen defenseless children and three or four teachers, you would move heaven and earth to do that! If you had two firebugs in your attic with many gallons of gasoline ready to torch your house, you would act immediately to stop them! If you knew that a passenger was about to board your plane with a powerful bomb in his briefcase you would move heaven and earth to stop that person before they boarded the plane! This list could go on ad infinitum but everyone by now must get the point! There are heinous, horrific disasters that have been carefully planned by the MAGA GOP well in advance that are impossible to stop or divert with a bi-annual vote or court actions that take six months to years to even convene!

If some form of law enforcement saw a madman carrying an AR-15 try to enter a school, he would shoot that person immediately - if not to kill, he would aim to at least completely disable that person. The downside result is just that dire! There would be no waiting for a court to incarcerate him. Perhaps, it would be better to eliminate every AR-15 available to such madmen. We now know that even passing such a law is essentially impossible and not very effective!

164   When a society is dealing with normal citizens that tend to obey laws, and that have an interest in keeping the beneficial 'status quo' that has prevailed for hundreds of years - laws, courts and voting are the ways that generally work to maintain that sane comfort and satisfaction. However, when the nation is facing a group of people - A kind of deliberate National Crime Syndicate - that have not only vowed to destroy the Democracy of America, but have further pledged a solemn loyalty oath to the Syndicate Crime Boss instead of an oath of allegiance to defend the Constitution of the United States and the Rule of Law, there is a definite crisis for Democracy very much like a madman with an AR-15 approaching a school building full of innocent children!!

These people are single minded and dedicated to a singular task and outcome that is not the preservation of the beneficial laws and traditions of this great land. Abnormal processes must be substituted to kill this sinister cancer before it even comes near the point of destroying this great nation. The world knows that these kinds of actions should have been taken in the 1930's to stop Hitler's rise to absolute power. Perhaps they did not know that then, but we do have the wisdom of history to inform us of what we must do now to prevent that very same demise from happening here in America! Bottom line: it absolutely doesn't include letting any of these Terrorists could run for office or to hold any office, either current or in the future. Even If abnormal processes are required to do that - it absolutely must be done. Just like the terrible importance of preventing a gunman killing 20 school children, it is far more important to preserve this democracy of 350 million people. By no stretch of imagination, as horrible and insane it is for anyone to slaughter 30 innocent children, it is thousands of times worse to destroy the lives and freedoms of 350 million citizens for centuries to come! To have even 0.0001% odds of this being able to happen is far too risky. A ZERO chance of this is the only acceptable odds!

Let me be extremely blunt! Even if Democrats take the House, Senate and the Presidency in 2024 we are not out of the woods by a very long shot. Too many years transpired before Merrick Garland and the DOJ moved one muscle to go after any of the top brass of the MAGA Crime Syndicate. If we lose this Nation as a Democracy, number one on the list to blame will be the delinquent AG of the DOJ. To save a nation from a well-planned and organized National Crime Syndicate required immediate action that would be both dramatic and very decisive. Top brass needed to be thrown in jail just as if they had been Foreign Terrorists that may have attacked the Pentagon. Treason and an Insurrection committed by tens of thousands in an armed mob must be dealt with swiftly and very decisively. There is absolutely no way that we would have wasted two years before going after the surviving perpetrators of an attack on the twin towers or the pentagon. No way, Jose!

Let me list just a few of the most treacherous things that this Crime Boss has committed in only the last four years. Any one of these would put a normal citizen in jail almost immediately, in most countries around the world including the America.

Stealing more than 100 secret and top-secret documents from the government. Some of these were so sensitive that they were never allowed outside of an extremely secure skiff and those that were allowed to view them had to have every kind of storage device taken from them before entering the skiff. There are people that have taken some documents home that are residing in a jail cell until trial for just taking one. This is considered by our government as being one of the highest crimes against our nation's security, affecting national defense or our foreign relations. The punishment may entail jail time of up to five years for each incident. Yet the crime boss is out on the golf course and campaigning for an office that he has clearly shown that he must NEVER be able to obtain!

166 He envisioned, planned and fully executed a plan to storm the Capitol building with an armed, overwhelming force of thousands of members of a mob. Many were there because he asked them to be there, and it would be wild. A smaller set was organized and focused on a para-military formation to ensure that the break in and penetration was done relatively quickly and totally effectively. Some members had the advantage of having MAGA congressional cohorts give guided tours of the tunnels and other intricacies of the Capitol building several days before the totally planned onslaught. This would give them and the mob the total advantage of knowing exactly where they were and how to get to the offices of key members of the "opposition traitors" as well as the House and Senate chambers to interrupt the count of the Electoral College ballots. This was a full-blown attempt to commit an armed Insurrection intended to overthrow the legitimate government of the United States. I don't know what you may call this, but in my book, I would call it TREASON!

If this armed insurrection were not enough, there were a half dozen other, separate, attempts that were simultaneously in operation to throw out the true outcome of the election to the Crime Boss instead. Complete slates of fraudulent 'electors' were named in seven different swing states to give the House an alternate set of MAGA electors to count instead of the real ones. These fraudulent electors signed their names to fake documents and mailed them to the congress and to the National archives. There are two words that criminally apply to that action and those are 'Mail Fraud'! Why in Hell wasn't the Postal Inspectors force sent to these homes (after this travesty was discovered) to arrest every one of them for committing mail fraud? Go figure that one out. Very Simple!

There were serious discussions about sending military forces to confiscate voting machines throughout the nation. Some machines were tampered with in Coffee County, GA.

There was a plan called the Green Bay Sweep that was an elaborate scheme to involve State governors or legislatures to "just find 11,780 votes" to make the tally come out to the Crime Syndicate Boss' advantage. That whole scheme is far too elaborate to detail here or currently. Nonetheless it was a way to overthrow the legitimate outcome of the election by an illegitimate set of actions. The list of criminally charged actions that were planned and implemented are mind boggling. Any one of them would be totally disqualified to allow the instigator to even be eligible to run for any office. So why is he running? Why is he allowed to run? Section three of the 14th amendment must disqualify him automatically for even any one of these high crimes and misdemeanors.

When it comes to his antics outside the various courts that he must attend, he must be severely sanctioned. The only one that makes sense to him is to be slammed into jail for the duration. There is no compelling reason why he must be campaigning or running for any office. He simply does not have any obligation to do any of those things. However, he absolutely must follow the rules of a federal court or any other court, for that matter. Petulant children must be disciplined especially after the authority has stated that they must desist from further abhorrent behavior, and they deliberately continue performing in the prior loathsome manner. The consequences of failing to follow through are extremely dangerous to the rule of law and the future of the Democracy of the United States. As bad as it may seem, it must be done to save the nation.

This country is at a dangerous impasse, and it cannot be saved at this point by just Kumbaya, votes or extremely slow courts. Certain decisive actions must be taken to shorten the time frame of action so something more reasonable has to be done to save the Nation so that true Democracy has time to survive. One form may be Marshal law to fix the House and the 168 voting. Here is, by far, the most frightening part of what is going on under all our noses and we are not even paying proper attention to it. These things are so sinister and deadly dangerous that they must be identified immediately, and actions taken to totally stop these destructive movements. The first of these is the equivalent to the Berlin Book Burning that happened during Hitler's rise to absolute power. So many state governments and errant school boards are involved in a fever pitch effort to ban books that the conservatives seem to find objectionable. They often include either black or LBGTQ authors or subjects. The supreme court has ruled that the banning of books is unconstitutional according to the first amendment of the constitution that guarantees the freedom of speech. This would also apply to music, plays, movies, lectures, art, photographs, etc. Without this fundamental guarantee we would soon cease to be a free society and would be, rather, an Authoritarian form of fascism.

But here's the rub. In general, this onslaught to democracy cannot be stopped by a vote, or an arrest. Too often the constitution doesn't provide any real teeth to stop action of this kind of constitutional violations. As a result, well organized constitutional terrorists are taking over school boards, library boards, voting boards, police departments and town halls. There, they are wreaking havoc on our democracy with total immunity and impunity. A lot of this process has been accomplished through intimidation and threats to one's jobs, lives or families. Oh my, this sounds way too similar with the growth of Nazism in Germany before WWII. It should have stopped very early there, but disastrous, it wasn't. Even though intimidation is against every state law, no one seems to be doing anything to stop it. That is a huge mistake. Also, faux militias are illegal in every state of the Union as well as the United States. Why aren't all these people being rounded up and arrested? So much needs to be done RIGHT NOW that just isn't getting done. We are IN FOR IT if we don't!

A last-minute edit and epiphany. Saturday, 10/7/23, Hamas 169 militants sent three thousand rockets and manned paragliders into Israel as part of a multi-faceted surprise attack against Israel. It was a complete shock to Israel that had no warning that anything like this was possible. It was a three-pronged attack by air, land and water. Members of the Hamas forces breached the barrier fences and kidnapped hundreds of Israeli hostages and took them back into the Gaza Strip for their own self-protection. Much worse than this, 1400 Israelis and 30 Americans were killed in Israel. Women were raped and citizens and children were beheaded and shot or burned in their homes, cars and at folk festivals, schools and kibbutzim. It was an all-out assault on the very essence of the Society of the State of Israel. It was an attempt to destroy Israel.

It is interesting that the MAGA GOP are calling Hamas out as being Terrorists. The irony is that these same MAGA GOP are not calling the thousands of deadly force insurrectionists that battered their way into our Capitol on 1/6/21 with the intent to kill the Vice President and perhaps 200 or 300 members of Congress as terrorists. They claim that they were just tourist visitors on a tour of the Capitol. I believe that may be the very definition of hypocrisy! The entire world saw both events and would not hesitate to classify both groups as terrorist events!

The October 7th war on Israel MUST BE a resounding wake up call for America! What makes Israel's war so obvious, and resounding is its suddenness, unexpectedness, and the brutality and horrific attack upon all of humanity. The atrocities are so beyond the pale that they are inconceivable even within today's tolerance for horror and brutality in our movies and other media. It is that "so much horror is such a short period of time" has forced worldwide attention and condemnation of it so universally. It has captured worldwide news for weeks. It was so gross that Israel has vowed to take out Hamas by the root and branch for all time. That is the war 170. that the world agrees

170 that Israel must have and to complete. There seems to be total agreement, from our own President, that this must be done. The same is true for the war to defeat Russia in Ukraine. These are two villains that must be defeated, root and branch, lest they and the world's democracies will be at total risk. It doesn't matter the cost!

It's time for all this BS in the news, and "political campaigns" to stop. For at least a decade, the United States has been under attack inside its borders by terrorists no less worthy than those from Hamas or from Trump's buddy, Putin's Russia. The "myriads of rockets" has already taken out our schools, universities and "woke" Magic Kingdom festivals in Florida, Texas. Tennessee and perhaps a dozen other strategic states in the nation. They are taking down our libraries, our polling places, voting booths and chief voting officials or secretaries of state in dozens of our sovereign States.

WE ARE AT WAR! NO less so than Israel or Ukraine is from Russia! We must start reacting as if we had been attacked like Israel or the Ukraine by Russia. The terrorist "rockets" have taken out many of our courts, including SCOTUS, the House and part of the Senate of our Congress, many library boards, school boards, local town, city and State Governments. Are very freedoms have been attacked and severely compromised. These include the freedom of speech and expression in books,

drama, arts, plays, music, entertainment, and the ability to converse freely with others. Our ability to be taught the entire truth about our history and aspects of our development are at total risk in dozens of states. The sanctity of science to protect us from harmful drugs and foods is under direct attack. Climate science has been hit with a total barrage of terrorist rockets and it is at risk of letting our planet die under sea from melted polar caps, glaciers and heat. It's time to take out the MAGA cancer by every root and branch and destroyed. There can be no compromise in this! We must have our Democracy!!
Some examples of how America has been attacked.   171

The First upon our Capitol on January 6ᵗʰ, 2021

The Second upon our Courts and especially SCOTUS

Military and Police

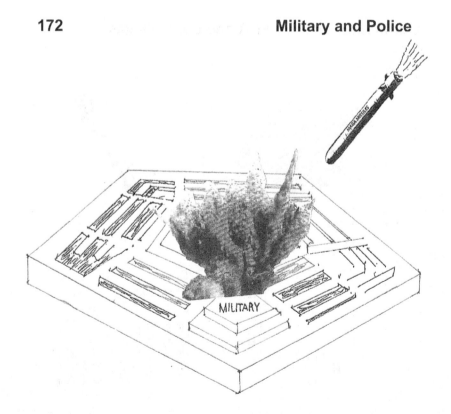

Third upon our Military

POLICE and FBI

Fourth upon our Police and FBI

Our Institutions like FDA and our Colleges   173

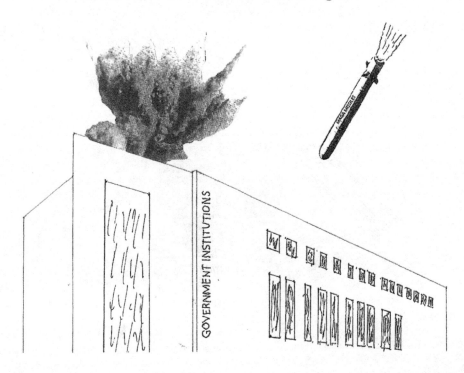

GOVERNMENT INSTITUTIONS

Fifth upon Government Institutions like the FDA

Sixth upon Colleges like in Florida

Schools and Libraries

Seventh upon our Schools

Eighth on our Libraries and Freedom of Speech and Thought

176   OK, YOU ASKED! SO HERE IS HOW IT TURNS OUT! Largely, until now, I've been telling you how this Catastrophe for America and thus the entire world will be implemented with a modicum of warnings about why this outcome is not to be desired. But, if you didn't live during WWII or, Heaven forbids live in North Korea, Russia, Turkey or during the present war in Ukraine, you really don't have a clue about how lifeless you and your family's lives will be if the Clown show at the head of the MAGA National Crime syndicate gets elected next November 2024. Having lived through WWII, I know a lot of what it was like, even though living relatively safely in America. I also know a few people who lived in Berlin. And Yugoslavia during that war and had many discussions about the atrocities that were part of everyone's miserable lives throughout the late 30s and early 40s in Germany and in Europe. I capitalized EVERYONE's because it wasn't just the "vermin", (as Hitler called them - the same thing Trump recently called "those thugs of the Democratic Party that are oddly not only Communists, but Fascists as well") but also those that were card carrying members of the Nazi party who joined thinking that somehow that would save their families and them from the total misery imposed upon the entire Nation. Thus, I will start my tale about your horrific choice that you may make out of total ignorance of how upside down your lives will be if the MAGA CRIME BOSS somehow gets anywhere near the White House again.

First, no matter how you previously got your news, it will be eliminated or converted into a MAGA CRIME SYNDICATE propaganda machine! You will not be able to read, hear or see anything about local, national or international news that hasn't been censored and propagandized. It appears that the MAGA CRIME SYNDICATE may have already done this to the Spanish media outlet called Univision. This outcome has angered many

of the anchors and the former listeners of that news channel. This prospect not only angers a very large portion of the former viewers, it is also an extremely dangerous turn of events that weaponized and silences the Free Press. You know how effective Fox News is at slanting the news to favor one "would-be dictator" of the United States. Now, it appears that MAGA has co-opted Univision to slant lies to the Hispanic community so that votes are switched from Biden to Trump. As proof of this technique, I refer to the book America Dies when based upon Lies. ISBN 979-8-67923-548-9, 2020. Lies destroy TRUST faster than any other method known to man and erodes the rule of law, government institutions, voting, courts, Congress, FDA, FBI, Military, School Boards, teachers., books and every tradition that has kept this country running for centuries. It's a simple tool that literally destroys everything that anyone deems of value. The worst part is that it is extremely hard to combat. ("A lie can travel halfway

around the world while the truth is still putting on its shoes."
Mark Twain) This is just the start of your demise under MAGA
CRIME rule!

REQUIRED to JOIN, BELONG, PARTICIPATE, or OSTRACIZED

You will find that one of the next things that has suddenly
happened to you, or your family is an insidious, intrusive
pressure to "be part of the right frame of mind or belong to the
right group or philosophy". People that you may have thought
that you knew most of your life may be listening to you now
and reporting what you say to "THE PARTY". You will find.
(often, but not quite soon enough) that they have become part
of the MAGA way of thinking, and you are now at odds with
your old friends. If they still like you, they will start putting
pressure on you to buy into the CULT or subscribe to its
tenants and thereby support it. This can get REAL in a HURRY
when this happens at your place of work and the person you
work for is now part of the MAGA Crime Syndicate. At first you
will be asked to join the MAGA CULT, as it would be nice.
178   to have a copacetic environment so that workers can
smoothly get along with each other. You politely decline the
nice invitation. Then it starts to get ugly! It is now made very
clear that it wasn't your choice to say "no". You are now under
pressure to join, or your performance reviews may have
dramatic consequences. You may be written up as a worker
that has difficulty "working with others". You will start to be
"written up" for one thing after another - most of them have no
basis. When you complain, further demerits are added, "as it
IS NOW CLEAR that you ARE A TROUBLEMAKER and not a
TEAM PLAYER". Your salary suffers. No more raises or
bonuses. There definitely will be no chance for any
promotions. As this ugliness proceeds, new pressure is added
to join the MAGA movement, or you will be FIRED for cause. It
is made clear that if you are fired you will be blackballed, thus
making it very difficult or nearly impossible to get another job.

How do you like those options? Believe it, these things did happen to people in Nazi Germany.

It's not just in your job. At your church or synagogue, you might say something at coffee hour that eventually leads to your being ostracized or excommunicated. There is nothing more devastating to your persona or psyche than suddenly not being able to talk to any of your former friends or, worse, they're choosing not to talk to you. This could happen in any club or organization to which you formerly belonged. Now we get to the nitty gritty. What about your family? YOUR FAMILY! One or two members may have joined the MAGA CULT. They can stop talking to you as well. In some cases, that may be a good thing, but, ah, I digress. No, I mean it! A family in that kind of turmoil and distress is a very devastating experience for anyone. Ah, all of this can be far more sinister than previously described. If you are in any of these situations and you are unaware that your boss, your minister, or your son or daughter have joined the MAGA CULT, they may be spying on you and reporting the views and comments that you have freely made to the MAGA CULT authorities so that they Can take "appropriate action" against you. For example: in Germany, one day you might just disappear and never be found or perhaps, at the least, end up in a concentration camp. DO NOT FORGET! Trump has been promising just such treatment for his "enemies list", and that includes anyone who spoke out against him at any time or were part of his team or CULT that sees the light and testifies against him. Yes, even if you might have been MAGA CULTISTS, you are not immune from this or any dictator's vengeance and retribution! He is not being devious anymore. He is spelling out his designs in very vivid and explicit detail. "I am your vengeance and your retribution!" If you go after me, I will go after you tenfold. For those who know history, these are the very plans used by Hitler to take over and control the citizens of Germany in the 1930s and 1940s.

Believe me, there's nothing here to play with or be cute about. This monster is a Crime Boss, a Terrorist. He means every word that he has spoken and printed in his Manifesto Project for 2025. They have organizing committees working every day on the plan to take over America and to destroy the Constitution and our beloved Democracy. How would you like to have your front door busted in at 3:00 in the morning and a loved one, or you, grabbed from bed by force and take it away, never to be seen - just like what Hamas did in Israel on October 7th, 2023. They are at war now, and we should be no less at war against the MAGA National Crime syndicate then Israel is against Hamas. PERIOD! There's nothing more to say!

WEAPONIZATION of the DOJ: Just one of the things on this Nazi inspired path to destruction of our Freedoms and our Democracy is a stated threat to totally weaponize the DOJ! You have already noticed that the MAGA movement, with a very slim majority in the House, has weaponized the committees. It may seem to be just political to go after Hunter Biden now, but
180   the tenant is to go after political opponents to try to discredit them before the pending elections in 2024. That means that by discrediting Hunter, the damage will fall upon the Biden family and the "Family Name" to diminish Joe's chances of winning the 2024 election. They are very short on actual necessary legislation to aid the war in Ukraine against the Putin invasion or to deal with serious domestic matters for the people of the United States. If their goal is to take down the entire democracy - starting with, not funding the government - they are well on that path by their deliberate actions or inactions. These are just precursors to their end.

Yes, it has been planned to get far more sinister than just the politics of these actions. The Project 2025 spells out how the president plans to fire everyone in the DOJ that they consider to be part of the Deep State. He will then hire a large cadre of sycophant supporters that they are testing and interviewing now to determine the extent of their loyalty to Donald Trump. These "ASS lickers" will be totally subservient to his whims, wishes and desires. They will, by then, have sworn an oath of loyalty to His Majesty - HERR FUHRER - the Dictator of the former United States of America. They, and the entire DOJ, will then become his personal enforcer of his Vengeance and Retribution upon everyone, and I do mean EVERYONE, of the huge crowd of people that the Fuhrer deemed to have slighted him from the least to the most! This would then be his equivalent of the Gestapo, S.S. or Brown Shirts of the 1930s.

He intends to defund the IRS so that the rich can become distinctively the very ugly rich. And the rest of you schmucks? You all get the triple size bill! He intends to defund the FDA, or perhaps eliminate it entirely. That way they can destroy America's ability to successfully fight the next 'COVID-19' like plague. They will stop science from its goal to save millions of lives and will stop all climate control funding or activities. We are not through with the destruction of your lives or freedoms that you take for granted and have enjoyed all   181 your lives. By either defunding or eliminating every Regulatory agency that has been protected. You from bad drugs, bad medicines or fruits or vegetables, that some field worker has said or peed upon, or sprayed with poisonous insecticides, you may be. Eating things from the store that may either make you very sick or kill you outright. Oh yes, so you now need to go to a hospital or immediate care. Good luck with that. Even though they would have you believe that they are for deregulation and a total reduction in the size of the government, you will find that none of these things are true. They fully expect to regulate the hell out of your life in every way that 1) you would never expect and 2) not in 1000 years do you ever want to have that happen to you or your family members.

They are already regulating your sex lives and medical health outcomes. They will be putting far more stringent restrictions upon what your doctor may do, or what doctors in the hospital or emergency rooms may be allowed to do without being arrested and convicted for countering one of their new wacky laws. Do you think that I'm trying to be funny or ridiculous? Just look at the Dobbs V Jackson decision ruled by SCOTUS on June 24th, 2022! Just look at what has already happened in Florida, Texas and a half a dozen other MAGA Crime Syndicate states. The law in Texas harkens back to the dark ages and the days of westward expansion in the United States. Vigilantes! The law empowers ordinary people - could be anyone that and doesn't have to be from Texas - to go after anyone that they deem has committed some portion of attempting to obtain an abortion. They can sue those people for $10,000 and expect to win the judgment! They can even go after taxi drivers who took the person to an airport or drove them across a state line to get an abortion. This kind of criminal indictment by law for doing what you have done your entire life is

182   forcing doctors to leave the state or to quit the profession entirely. WHAT's NEXT? Let's put it this way. These kinds of laws were in abundance in Hitler's Germany and are very prevalent in places like Putin's Russia or Kim Jong-un's North Korea. What do you think the consequences are for laws that fine you, put you in jail, or execute you for either doing something or not doing something that has been prescribed by the law? Many of the forbidden things are things that you have done and enjoyed your entire lives. Does any of that sound like you're being able to live the life that you would enjoy? Hell no! Twenty thousand Russians have been jailed in the past two years for even mentioning the word WAR since the war with Ukraine started two years ago. They are serving 7-to-15-year sentences. Now how does that get your family's bills paid?

In Florida, you can't say the word, Gay. You can't read certain books that a select group of people have decided would be detrimental to your further existence. Nice of them to be so concerned for your welfare. Frankly, I'd rather keep that choice for myself and for my children. That's the equivalent to "the stench of a Berlin book burning". That goes against every precept of this Democracy's "Freedom of Speech". You don't have to wait for Trump to be in office to be subject to those violations of our Constitution to occur. They are already being imposed in some 32 states of the union as this book is being written in 2023. Book banning has more than doubled in just the past year. Books like movies, drama, music and other forms of art and expression, are a foundation of our Constitution and are not to be abridged. This is one of the first things that a Fascist Autocratic Dictatorship does to control the thoughts and minds of their "imprisoned population". This "in spades" is what everyone living in the United States must look forward to if Trump is allowed to be elected. It is essentially impossible to erase such radically destructive alterations to our Rights and Freedoms guaranteed by the Constitution once destroyed in this manner. It took many   183 free allies, A brutal four-year war to defeat Hitler! SCHOOLS: How many of you are looking forward to having your children going to schools where they will be forced to memorize MAGA Crime Syndicate Fascist ideologies, like hordes of children in the Middle East repeating dogma repeatedly as if they are in a Madrasa school? Believe me, it is not a pretty sight to see heads bobbing up and down as they repeat a phrase repeatedly to get it thoroughly entrenched into their skulls. We have Florida to thank for this kind of horrific aberration of public education. They are already taking over school boards and administrators of public schools and universities to remove all "dangerous liberal ideas and subjects" from the curriculum.

They have removed boards of directors and Provost of public universities and replaced them with rabid fascist automatons. These administrators have removed all liberal thinking teachers and replaced them with automaton instructors. They have eliminated every subject that does not fit within their narrow line of ideology and propaganda. Guess how this turns out when a hapless graduate wants to go on to an accredited Graduate School for an advanced degree. These colleges haven't a ghost of a chance to be accredited by any respected accreditation organization. Whatever career your student thought that he may have, is now completely dead from the start. Try to get a real job? Boy, there's a laugh! From that school? Are you F--king kidding me? Go work at a fast-food outlet if you think that they will hire a "college graduate" from one of those schools. Good luck on that one as well.

What ideologues never ever figure out is that when you believe something that is so entirely wacko with reality that it can never ever work, you will sooner or later end up with the dire consequences of a system that will ultimately fail. These are based upon some abstract principle that has been totally.
184   created in the fanciful vacuum of some nut-job's mind. Nut-jobs never ever work out the details to make theories work. What follows now is the severe damage that a MAGA Crime Syndicate will be doing to your children before and after school. The Nazis either forbade the Boy Scouts or co-opted it to be a youth indoctrination Corp where young minds could be filled with loyalty to Germany and Der Fuhrer. These youth corps were both training camps for military indoctrination and propaganda camps for shaping the mindset of the next up and coming generation. This was a way that Hitler Youth could turn a Generation of kids into Nazis. Hitler's war against the Boy Scouts fueled the Third Reich's ideology - and its military might. ("How the Hitler Youth Turned a Generation of Kids into Nazis" By Aaron Blakemore. Updated June 29th, 2023, The Original: December 11th, 2017)

There was a far more sinister group we know as the Brown Shirts but were known in Germany as the Sturmabteilung or SA (Assault division). The word Sturm is translated as storm, but in this case loosely has the meaning of attack or assault. Abteilung, in military nomenclature, is a 'division'. They were otherwise known as Storm Troopers. This group of young men were at first a loosely formed group of enforcers, much as we now know as the Three Percenters, the Proud Boys, or the Oath Keepers. They were largely used to disrupt political or. civic meetings, private clubs or business organizations similar to Kiwanis, Lions or Rotary clubs. They were also used to create terror in the minds of any opposition movements or members that were perceived to 'threaten' the ideals of the Nazi Party. They were sent to destroy businesses of people that the Nazi regime had labeled as enemies, such as Jewish businesses. One of their prime roles was that of being intimidators of undesirable people. Or groups of people. If you don't think this can happen here, you simply have not been paying attention. What do you think happened at the Capitol on 1/6/21? What do you think is happening to ordinary people that Der Fuhrer has singled out to be traitors, like the two 185 election workers in Georgia that have been threatened and tormented after the 2020 presidential election? Their lives have been in shambles ever since that intimidation. Trump stated that he will go after every one of his enemies!

COURTS: Boy, watch out for this sleeper, this deadly attack that generally scuttles under the radar can be deadly when the true magnitude of its unholy terror descends upon the otherwise normally sane, majority of the population. You see, when the legislature loses its way and passes totally insane, abusive, restrictive laws that take away the freedoms or rights that were bound to the public by the Constitution or other previously enacted beneficial laws, the public has the power of the vote to remove those terrorist elements from the lawmaking legislatures. It takes time, but there is at least a possible remedy to eventually have a chance to correct the situation. On the other hand, if a court rules that something that everyone has enjoyed their entire life is no longer valid or available for use - it is curtains for that freedom of right. We do not vote to place judges in courts and their tenure is almost always for life. We do not have a Democratic process by which to change that outcome. Courts tend to be the very last word.

So, let us look at some recent examples of how bad this use of the courts can be. These are examples that have already occurred as a result of MAGA leaning judges, many of whom were appointed by President Trump. A MAGA, leaning judge in Texas was "judge shopped" by a group of MAGA influenced doctors that were trying to eliminate the use of mifepristone. Mifepristone is preferred to be used in combination with misoprostol as a two-step Process to end a pregnancy. However, the drug has far more valid uses as prescribed that do not involve the end of a pregnancy. This drug is used many times a day in OBGYN sections of hospitals. The irony is that God causes far more abortions than doctors by artificial
186 means. About 2.5% of pregnant women have induced abortions, where about 40% of pregnant women have natural miscarriages. It is primarily for this reason that banning a drug just because you may be opposed to its use in abortion is not a wise decision because it is a very necessary drug for saving the lives of women for far more naturally occurring reasons. Here's another way courts have been used to subvert normal situations in a way to greatly abort real justice. When an ideologue has appointed a MAGA indoctrinated or MAGA leaning Judge, there may be a time when that judge may be in a crucial position to subvert normal justice. Such a case has occurred in Florida in relation to a case against the MAGA leader that was so obvious that it would be a slam dunk in any court in the land. That judge, who was appointed by the MAGA leader defendant, did everything to either stop or slow down

that trial or to put roadblocks before to try to completely nullify the charges. The dangerous part is that those judges generally have the last word in their courtrooms. So, if they are able to abort justice, by one of a dozen means, the results tend to be non-reversible to be consistent with justice. This, and many more examples, shows why dictators almost always try to appoint their own "loyal" judges as soon as they can in their quest for total control of a government.

Now, here's the part that absolutely gives me shivers every time I think about it - currently, that is many times a day! Why do we have a District Court if an Appellate Court exists? Why do we have an Appellate Court if the Supreme Court exists? OK, perhaps you didn't get the reasoning behind this dilemma. When someone has clearly committed a crime that is demonstrably provable by universally known facts, you would expect that the first trial in the 1st court would serve to lock that person up for the known crime that he has committed. So that court, with a jury, convicts him of a crime and the sentence is 10 years in a federal prison. It should be DONE, FINI, OVER, slam dunk - the court has ruled - he goes to jail.
Perhaps that is what would happen to 99% of us, but why 187 Is it possible to "get out of jail" cards for rich or influential people? What in hell is a District Court for if you can just decide that you don't like the outcome and go to the Appellate Court to beg for your "get out of Jail" card? The same goes for that court when you go to SCOTUS for a "get out free" card.

A DIFFERENCE BETWEEN a DICTATOR and a DEMOCRACY: Hopefully, you now have a feel for how dire things will be for everyone if a MAGA Crime Syndicate Boss is elected to the White House in 2024. EVERYONE, this is deadly serious! This election ISN'T about AGE or the detriment that has been projected and propagandized for Biden's years of experience! It is VERY CLEARLY about everyone's freedoms, rights, and opportunities that they have enjoyed their entire lives and are fully expecting to continue for many generations to come. Why would anyone suspend their senses long enough to willingly give up the lives of their families and those of generations to come? IT JUST DOESN'T MAKE ANY SENSE! In fact, it's totally insane. These rights, opportunities and freedoms will be lost forever if the people of America are "worn down" enough to lack judgment to elect a "Hitler-like" Fascist, Nazi, AUTOCRATIC DICTATOR like Germany did in the 1930s!!

The thing about history is that it can and does foretell a dire future for America if it does not heed its absolute warnings of total disasters to the Democracy of the United States. If one ignores the Lessons of history, they're bound to repeat them with their very lives! I realize that most of you didn't live then, but you can read books, pay attention to history classes in school, or just watch a documentary or two about how terrible those years were for EVERONE in the world! The absolute bottom line? There can be only one dictator, and I guarantee it that it will not be any one of you - whether MAGA or not! EVERYONE will suffer under the cruel vengeance of a SUPER NARCISSISTIC, MISOGYNISTIC, TREASONOUS MANIAC!

188   THE BOTTOM LINE: In these 12 pages, I have attempted to present just a modicum of the excruciating HORRORS that will besiege you almost immediately after the 2024 election if you have not paid any attention to history or these dire warnings. Believe me, I have only exposed the tip of the iceberg on these pages! Read history or watch a few documentaries and you will get a far better feel for the depths of depravity that would suddenly afflict you. Just like in SUDDEN THEORY, a life that you have enjoyed all your years - IN AN INSTANT - suddenly turns to SH-T. The awful thing about SUDDENESS is that you absolutely have no warning. Just like a car accident. One moment you are alive, the next you are dead. Your life changes in microseconds!

Unless you are a mentalist that can foretell the future, are you able to predict your fate? That is why we have the advantage of horrendous insights from one of the worst periods of our past created by one of the most sinister people on earth - Adolf Hitler. We have apparently met his 21st century psychotic sycophant that now resides in America. Since this person is hell bent upon duplicating his mentor's worst nightmares, we have, through history, a very clear road map to what will afflict all of us if we are not mindful of that terrible history. Take full advantage of everything that you can find about that awful period and immediately apply it to actions to avert an already well-planned repeat of that kind of demise for your lives. Ironically, this MAGA Crime Boss also has the advantage of knowing that terrible history and has been using it to plan your awful demise for a decade!

How many meetings has the Democratic Party had to plan and anticipate proactive measures to avert this horrible end to our Democracy as we know it? I would guess less than 5! Wake up America! This demise has been upon us for at least a decade. The media has just become aware of the dangers. EVERYONE must now pull together to prevent this outcome!

WOULD YOU VOTE FOR HITLER IF YOU KNEW NOW
WHAT YOU KNOW ABOUT HITLER?
WOULD YOU VOTE FOR PUTIN IF YOU KNEW NOW,
WHAT YOU KNOW ABOUT PUTIN?
THEN WHY WOULD YOU CONSIDER VOTING FOR TRUMP?
So why am I asking these questions that seem so simple and innately obvious? It is because, even though it seems patently obvious to most rational, discerning people that this man is so flawed that he makes Hitler seem like a saint. It turns out that there is a very large part of the population that is tone deaf to his alarming lies and his constantly hateful din! You might give them the benefit of the doubt that they were just born idiots. But no! Many of them were Trump haters from day one and said so vehemently many, many times. Many were solid

citizens, albeit politicians, that would never have followed this Pied Piper anywhere years ago. Many were so "on to him" that they have ruthlessly called him out about his being totally unfit to represent anything - especially the United States!

Do you remember George W. Bush, who incidentally acted as the candidate that co-opted religious rights into taking over the Conservative GOP party? This was done despite his father's supposed lack of interest in the goals of the Religious Right. This relationship led directly to today's Christian Nationalism! The roots to the demise that is staring 350 million Americans in the face started 12 to 16 years ago by people like Ronald Reagan and George W. Bush. It would have been pushed by Romney if he had been elected but was completely active under G. H. W. and G. W. Bush. Unfortunately, even though some of us recognized the dangers then, most of the population were lulled into thinking that these people were just being "normal" conservative Republicans. "They were just a bit of an annoyance but not really dangerous."

190 That having been said, Clarence Thomas was appointed to SCOTUS in 1991 by H. W. Bush. Talk about sleeper cells in a terrorist plot to take out someone or something very important in history; Clarence Thomas was just such a cell! For years his role in SCOTUS was the silent one who just sat like a frog on a log and asked no questions during court dissertations. Occasionally, he wrote opinions that belied his inner self, but otherwise he was pretty much an enigma. However, now, in just the past year, America has seen the treachery, the dramatic effect of the sleeper cell in Thomas, that was planted 33 years ago by a man who was then considered a true statesman, H. W. Bush.

It has been revealed that Clarence has taken almost $5 million in out and out bribes from rich donors that clearly have very dark and sinister agendas to promote and to be absolutely secured by actions of the highest court in the land! Irreversible decisions that already have impacted the lives of 350 million people very negatively, putting them in physical danger or even death. That is only the tip of the iceberg. In so doing, the Court has completely re-written the constitution or has destroyed its beneficial parts in such a way that Democracy itself will not be able to survive. Some of these rulings augment the absolute powers of an illegitimate dictator who intends to destroy the greatest Democracy in the world to satisfy Putin's sinister designs for the world. Traitors, ALL of them!!

Starting with McConnell's blockade of the ratification of Merrick Garland to SCOTUS during the last year of Obama's term (ten months before the end of Obama's term), Trump was able to pick three judges that had been handpicked by Leonard Leo and the Federalist society. Even though America was suspicious of the appointments of Samuel Alito (G. W. Bush), Neil Gorsuch, Brett Kavanaugh and Amy Coney Barrett (all three by Trump), they were totally ignorant of the 191 complete MAGA NATIONAL CRIME SYNDICATE takeover of the court until the now infamous Presidential immunity ruling that rewrote the Constitution of the United States.

Starting with the Dobbs ruling two years ago that ended 50 years of women's rights, it appeared that the court was doing something that it had never done in its entire life - overrule what is known as Stare Decisis - a court ruling that had been decided by SCOTUS years earlier. It removed the rights that had belonged to women for over 50 years. Then they followed that by overruling Section 3 of the 14th amendment to the constitution regarding whether an officer of the United States government, (i.e. The President) could be banned from any federal or state office because he materially broke his oath of office, and by doing nothing to stop a traitorous hours-long coup attempt to overthrow the US government on 1/6/21. This was a coup attempt that the President organized and implemented for his benefit alone! No one else on earth would benefit from that and there was not anyone else on earth evil enough, self-centered enough, or power hungry enough to even consider such a traitorous act to do nothing more than to appease his own greed and lust for power!

This person is so dangerously evil, to the extent that he is totally out of control and is so deviant to society that he must be locked up in jail or confined to a mental institution for the safety of all Democracies of the world. He is so dangerous that if he "wins" the presidency again, the democratic order of the world might be in danger of being destroyed forever!

I have recently read books that I wrote 12 and 16 years ago. These are books that were sent to both Obama and President Joe Biden at the time. As is often the case, I am shocked at the fact that these books not only were deadly accurate but literally predicted what has happened to America since then;
192   foretold exactly the situation that America finds itself in today with this race to eliminate the most dangerous dictator/ terrorist since Hitler, Mussolini or Tojo/Hirohito of Japan (Pearl Harbor, December 7, 1941). So much should have happened in the past decade to ward off this truly terrible progression towards a Fascist Autocratic Dictatorship that has been in the works of the GOP party for about two decades. (See PERFECT TRAP, Turnin A. Hausround 2012) (See Oh, Tyranny - Asymmetric Warfare - Key to Destruction, 2022)

It isn't for lack of forewarning by perhaps hundreds of authors that were able to analyze the terrible roadmap left by Hitler when he took over the Democratic Weimar Republic of Germany in 1933 and applied the essence of it to the present day. One of these well-known authors is Timothy D. Snyder of Yale University. Another author with an extremely exacting definition of the history of the world's progressions to tyranny and the rise of strongmen is Ruth Ben-Ghiat at New York University. All of these, and perhaps hundreds more, foretold and warned "the reading world" of the very real dangers of the rise of just such dangerous men and not only how to recognize them early enough to take decisive actions against them, but also to warn about the terrible effects these terrorists will have on everyone's lives for essentially forever if they are not stopped completely before gaining the real power that they constantly seek. We have done so little to heed these very accurate warnings, to plan for and to take drastic measures to head these terrorists off at the pass, and to cut out this very deadly cancer before it completely metastasizes. After twenty years, it may be a little too late to end it effectively. Drastic action should have already been taken but must be taken NOW!!

Hopefully, you will have picked up the subtle reference to "the reading world". Key to the survival of every working society is being effectively informed about what is happening in and to the world around them. Yes, there are recordings, radio, 193 and TV, but the printed page is unique in that it allows everyone to "hear" at their own pace and on their own time and duration of their choosing. If those precious words are removed from view or are just outright forbidden - that is the beginning of the end of entire civilizations! That is why, when a dozen people go around the country and instigate the banning of not just any books, but every book related to "objectionable" history, thought, ideologies, freedom of expression, or real stories about heroism, trauma, sadness, joy and love, look out! The end of your meaningful life must be very close behind!

One of the first lessons of the rise of Nazism in Germany was the Berlin Book Burnings. The second lesson was that it was not effectively stopped by those most affected and thus led to the rapid fall of that civilization. Our lesson is that we Must Not and Cannot let this atrocity go unchecked here in America, or our children and young adults will be left to mediocrity in thought and deed. When you ban books, it is to narrow the "experience" to just the dogma and indoctrination that the dictatorial society wants to propagate to their entrapped population. It is mind-warping and total indoctrination. In Germany, it was Nazism. In America, it is MAGA National Crime Syndicate Propaganda, White Supremacy and White Christian Nationalism dogma. Can anyone imagine getting an advanced degree in a censored university where you are taught subjects that are not translatable to earning a living or being accredited to continue in any meaningful endeavor in life? What a total waste of time in a college and what a total loss of spectacular achievements in science and technologies for all of mankind. The door might as well be closed to everything that is good and meaningful, and just shut the entire planet down. Why would anyone want to live under a dictatorship?

194   Since the last edition of this book so much has happened in America that simply goes beyond all belief and stretches credulity to the very limit of everyone's tolerance. My God, nobody could make this stuff up unless he was a mad narcissist working on a movie set - or in a real nut house. ("One Flew Over the Cuckoo's Nest" kind of a place - Ken Kesey, 1962) For starters, just think of the thousands (perhaps millions) of hours of literally pure nonsense that has been propagated to America by essentially an irrelevantly lying bastard that has demanded the world's attention to produce exactly nothing of any value for civilization or mankind. It is just pure garbage!

Then, there are the (perhaps millions of) hours totally wasted by the news media trying to follow this nonsense and trying to make some sense out of it! They have wasted my valuable time as well as all your valuable time just putting up with this total garbage. He is not really part of a legitimate party as it concerns actual elections performed in the United States. He is the head of either a National (or International) Crime Syndicate. There is nothing legitimate about his ability to run for any office in this country. He is a 34-time convicted felon and represents every avarice, deceit, illegitimate activity known to mankind and has no redeeming value to either society or to mankind. In effect he represents the lowest form of bottom feeders, mud suckers, despicable derelicts the world has ever known! (Mark 7:22-24 New Revised Standard Version Updated Edition: "Adultery, avarice, slander, deceit, debauchery, wickedness, envy, pride, folly. All these things come from within, and they defile a person.") To all of those totally emaciated, emasculated men (and women) who are sycophantically clinging to his every pronouncement and word - good luck to you! You, by your fawning, have lost your souls and are doomed to go down and be consumed in a lake of fire (Revelations 20:13-15). If you are the Christians that you claim that you are, you will fully understand the reference 195 to being foretold of an unfortunate end. You are these lost souls.

THE LAUGHINGSTOCK OF THE WORLD
He has stated several times that the United States is the laughingstock of the world! For perhaps the first time in his entire life he has told the truth. He is so fluent at lying that to tell the truth is a rare if totally non-existent and probably an uncomfortable experience for him. Yes, look at us!

What other country in the world lets a known terrorist, traitor, coup plotter, 34 times convicted felon, tax cheater, grifter, con man, self-serving opportunist to destroy the Constitution of

America and establish a horrible dictatorship in its place. Who allows that idiocy? He is so transparent about it that he announced a 920-page doctrine, called project 2025, that spells out the fullest details of his plan to destroy the democracy of America if he "wins the vote". That has got to be the very definition of the words, "TOTAL INSANITY"! Yes, who allows that form of ultimate stupidity and absolute Insanity? Every other country I know, if they can catch them, shoot or hang them for promulgating and inciting violence with the intent to overthrow their government. What inspires a group of people to basically pledge allegiance to the leader of a sworn enemy of your own country? Who does that? And in this well-informed day and age, who in HELL would, not just willingly but eagerly, opt to place an evil, self-serving, Narcissistic dictator in charge of their lives rather than the well-serving democracy that gave them every opportunity to enjoy their lives. A life that brought them to this point and to the fullest life that they have had till now. Isn't this the definition of total insanity? Damn right the world is laughing at us, but with tears, fear and trepidation that it may likely befall them as a result. They are terrified at the thought of another Hitler, or Mussolini being allowed to control a major democracy and ally in the world. We. all deserve far better than this. Unfortunately, 196 we let this maniac get control of our courts and faux militias while we looked the other way!

Doesn't it just make your skin crawl when someone who is pretending to be presidential, or at least would like you to believe that he is presidential, is selling cheap tennis shoes for $500 apiece just so that he and his family can grift off of the absolute stupidity of his sycophantic minions? That's just creepy! He's using every one of your poor slobs last $5 to line a millionaire's pockets. Do you have mansions in 6 or 7 places? Do you have one or two jet airplanes? How many golf courses do you own? He has them, but you never will! So why are you sending your very last nickel to support his GREED,

AVERICE and extreme Narcissism?! And for what? To get him back into a position of absolute power, so that he can just TAKE the MONEY instead of asking for it?! To take him to a place where he can assure that you lose your job so that you can never make a living after he takes all your remaining money and savings?! To a place where he can just have his private Gestapo roust you out of your bed in the middle of the night, throw you into a crowded concentration camp and throw away the key?!

He doesn't give a dime about your plight. Narcissists only care about themselves! Oh, the courts you say! Will you appeal to the courts to get your life restored? Oh, do you mean the MAGA courts, or the already MAGA SCOTUS? Have you been to Russia or North Korea and gotten on the wrong side of their view of good and evil? Well, just talk to Brittney Griner! See how that worked out for her. What about Alexei Navalny? They killed him in a prison in Siberia. No, I don't think so. This man's view of HIS new government Isn't just a difference of opinion about how things are or will be. He's not just a more conservative Republican than some that you have known. Hell, NO he isn't! His view of life is like nothing that anyone has ever experienced in his lifetime! And believe me, after one week or one month, you will be begging to go back to the 197 life you used to have. But guess what? Your wrong thinking vote has absolutely NO WAY BACK-FOREVER!

Yes, we are the laughingstock of the world in yet another terrible way! When I worked for companies that handled classified documents, I had to be investigated by the FBI to even get a SECRET clearance. Now, there are higher classifications like TOP SECRET and TS/SCI (Top Secret/ Sensitive Compartmentalized Information). Not only was there an investigation of our background, but we also had to attend classes on how to protect the documents that we might be 167 able to see or read and be forewarned about the

consequences if we were to break these very strict rules. Literally, if we took one document home, we could go to jail awaiting trial. These fall under statutes of 18 USC $ 793(e) or 18 USC $ 1924. The first deals with unauthorized possession of sensitive materials determined to be "related to the national defense". The second deals with the unauthorized removal of <u>classified</u> documents. Under this statute it is a crime for any officer of the United States Government to knowingly possess <u>classified</u> documents and to remove them without proper authorization. Penalties for violating both statutes include fines, imprisonment or both. The removal or possession of a non-classified document is covered by statute 18 USC $ 2071, section 2071(a). This is also punishable by being sent to prison. If I had taken just one classified document home, I would have been sent to jail. The ex-president both took home and possessed over 100 classified documents and stored them in plain sight in a bathroom and a ballroom of a very public resort in Florida - a place where 1000's of domestic and foreign visitors walked freely throughout the year. These documents were classified from secret to TS/SCI and included atomic secrets that fall under a special category of the National Defense act. These may be prosecuted directly because of their extremely sensitive nature related to our
198   national defense. TS/SCI documents must NEVER be outside of a SCIF without notification of a secure courier for safe transport to another SCIF. A public ballroom isn't secure nor is it a SCIF!

Here is part of the "laughingstock". This crime of stealing and possibly revealing dozens of top-secret documents should be a slam dunk! First, anyone else would have been in jail immediately after the discovery of just one stolen document, not over 100! Two, there is absolutely no need for any of these documents to be available for a trial. All that is needed is a list of the classifications of the stolen documents and how many were never to be outside of a secure SCIF. The court or court participants do not need to even know the titles of the documents, much less the contents! Three, almost any judge could have had this trial done within four months. It really is a slam dunk. It is a federal crime, punishable by imprisonment, to even possess these documents. There is sufficient A Priori evidence by the FBI raid that all these documents were not where they were supposed to be and were in fact in Trump's possession for a very long extended time long after he was notified that they must be immediately returned to the US Government for proper storage and security. Everything in that last statement is a Federal Crime.

The world is looking on in total disbelief that a federal judge is blatantly WORKING for the DEFENDANT in this trial! There has got to be a law against that! Who does that? Who does that so blatantly that a two-year-old intuitively knows that this cannot be allowed. JUDGES DON'T WORK for DEFENDANTS! The president with his newfound abilities, because of the SCOTUS immunity ruling, can just replace her - NOW! DO IT!

In what universe does a known traitor, insurrectionist, coup plotter, Fascist Autocratic Dictator, devout planner of the destruction of the United States Constitution with the complete ruination of 340 million lives, liar, crook, cheat, 199 thief, 34-times convicted felon, manage to thwart the entire US DOJ and justice system in at least 4 major trials for treason, and other federal crimes for over two years? Does that make the world laugh? It makes me cry out for the total ineptness of our judicial system. We truly are the laughingstock of the world! But they are not really laughing at us as they are so alarmed about the future of humanity, civilization, and all the world's Democracies that this travesty of justice is so freely allowed to happen.

America has got to get so fed up with this blatant corruption of Justice and dangerous harangue that they get up and root this

MAGA NATIONAL CRIME SYNDICATE out of effective existence and play in our national discourse. This total nonsense has just got to be ended, once and for all, for the very long foreseeable future. This kind of clattering DIN is making this fine nation a mere shadow of itself. Obviously, that is Putin's goal and Trump is Putin's idiot, Organ Grinder's Monkey Puppet! Watch him do the Monkey dance for his puppet master. Hear him praise him (Putin) loudly while bashing every other world leader other than Kim Jung-un. Hear him praise his puppet Judge Cannon in Florida, while he lambastes every other judge and prosecutor in every other court where he was to be tried. He is not very transparent! Just watch who he praises and who he tries to destroy with insults and derogatory remarks. That tells the world where his head is and what he intends to support and follow. Doesn't it bother all of you that he praises and supports Putin of Russia - our staunch adversarial enemy - not the people who are working to support America? In my book that is the very definition of TREASON. If he loves his country and him so much, why doesn't he just go there to live and take his entire MAGA CRIME SYNDICATE with him? They can all love and praise Putin from their jail cells!

200   What in HELL is wrong with Fani Willis? Her grand jury finished the case in January 2023. She could have indicted them by April 2023. Instead, she waited until late August. She could have finished the trial by October 2023. It is August 2024, and the trail hasn't even been scheduled. In the meantime, the defendants' lawyers have run circles around this trial, delaying it with investigations into Fani Willis. The trial should have been completed before any of these shenanigans could have ever happened. Yet another corruption of justice was completed, and justice totally denied by a clown, a buffoon, an Organ Grinder's Monkey, dancing on the end of a chain for pennies from Putin! Again, total justice denied. We are indeed the laughingstock of the world - a very

sad, bitter, and alarming laugh - filled with tears and trepidations!

Time to catch up on some of the most alarming history that we've seen in a lifetime. First, we will deal with the multiple trials that have been planned with a significant part of them in jeopardy of never occurring. The ex-president was facing about 88 charges in multiple court venues. The state trials seem to be far more effective than the federal trials. The bottom line in this, other than an apparent ineptness of the DOJ under Merrick Garland, seems to be due to the serious corruption of the MAGA SCOTUS. This court has done everything it could to either delay or overrule Trump's trials into oblivion. These decisions have defied every precept and legal opinion on constitutional law by 50 or more well-known constitutional lawyers.

For example, there is the totally bogus notion of absolute presidential immunity. In the 248-year history of the United States, no president has ever had presidential immunity after leaving office. Even immunity while in office is not in the constitution. (See ArtII.S3.5.1 Presidential Immunity to Suits and Official Conduct as spelled out in CONSTITUTION

ANNOTATED - under United States v. Nixon) In the two   201 centuries since the Burr trial, the executive branch's practices and Supreme Court rulings "unequivocally and emphatically endorsed" chief justice Marshall's position that the President was subject to federal criminal process. In its 2020 opinion in Trump v. Vance, the court extended this precedent to State criminal proceedings concluding that the President was not immune from state criminal subpoenas.

Yet, when prosecutor Jack Smith sent a brief to SCOTUS on 12/11/2023 asking SCOTUS to rule on Trump's absurd claim to absolute immunities, they refused to decide on that issue and sent it to the DC Circuit Court of Appeals on 12/11/2023 to decide the case. That court decided and ruled on 2/6/2024 in a 67-page judgement; that the ex-President is an ordinary citizen after leaving office and is therefore not immune to any prosecution - essentially no different than any other citizen. IE. No man is above the law - even an ex-President! (Page 3 of DC Circuit Court of Appeals ruling dated 2/6/24 No. 233228: *"Today we affirm the denial. For the purposes of this criminal case, former President Trump has become Citizen Trump, with all the defenses of any other criminal defendant. But any executive immunity that may have protected him while he served as President no longer protects him against his prosecution."*) That was a slam dunk! SCOTUS sent the request to the district court to decide the matter - essentially washing their hands of the case. The district court ruled absolutely in accord with 248 years of history and every other accepted precedent by the courts and impeachment cases in the House and Senate - THERE ARE NO and CANNOT BE any KINGs or Dictators in this Democracy! NO MAN IS ABOVE THE LAW - not even a Traitorous ex-president! Though it's been obvious to the entire world for centuries - even a two-year-old knows that giving one person immunity from all crimes, not only demolishes the RULE of LAW but allows that person to 202 be an Autocratic Authoritarian Dictator. That's not compatible with any Democracy.

Yet, guess what? Treasonous act upon Treasonous act, the MAGA SCOTUS then decided to take up the immunity issue (after refusing to do so when appealed to them in December 2023) and set the hearing for late in April 2024 for a decision on their very last day in session on July 1, 2024. Guess what, this entire shenanigan delayed the January case from the set date in March 2024 to - essentially NEVER! The MAGA

SCOTUS effectively delayed Chutkan's Jan 6 case from 12/11/23 to some months after 7/1/24. As of 8/1/2024, it has still not been decided if the case can proceed!

On July 1, 2024, SCOTUS re-wrote the Constitution and threw out 248 years of understanding and precedence to obviously serve the very criminal goals of their IDOL, the ex-President Trump. THERE CAN BE NO OTHER EXPLAINATION! The RULE OF LAW was essentially destroyed along with the Integrity and sanctity of the Constitution. Immunity, Dobbs and the Chevron Doctrine proves that SCOTUS has become a wholly owned MAGA Crime Syndicate Court! It must be declared as totally corrupt and disbanded pending a non-political committee establishing the names of thirteen nonpartisan a-political constitutional judges to be appointed by President Biden and ratified by the Senate! This nation cannot function or survive with a totally corrupt SCOTUS. It just must not stand! By being extremely partisan to a traitorous dictator means that every ruling will be directed toward the destruction of our nation and, thus, it will not be able to survive! This is an extreme example of Asymmetric Warfare and shows why it is so totally destructive to a Democracy.

Do you see what this MAGA SCOTUS has proved to the world in the past two years? It DOESN'T provide an independent and IMPARTIAL judgment about the meanings of the RULE of LAW or the Constitution! It proves what my books have said for 16 years. Never ever elect a GOP President that can stack the Court with Far-Right religious ideologists that can nullify any rule, law, measure put forward by Congress, or decisions of scientific departments that have been established to protect the American public! Here are examples such as FDA, DOJ, DO AG, DO COM. DOD, DOE, DO ENERGY, DO HEALTH, DO Homeland Security. A crime ridden, corrupt Court such as SCOTUS, can overrule everything our government does or provides for us and it is totally irreversible because there is no higher Court to supersede its opinions. Even Congress is not likely to be able to override its opinions.

Even a high school student can see that very plainly written and clear sections of the Constitution have been totally corrupted with entirely new meanings that are contrary to everyone's understanding. They have been written to favor traitors, Coup-planner, and insurrectionist! What is worse, they have been written in a way to help Implement Project 2025 and its White Christian Nationalist dogmas and Draconian Visions for America. Starting with the Dobbs decision ending abortion and ending with an extremely bizarre granting of absolute immunity for an ex-President that has been charged with 88 Federal crimes, there is no way that it can be said that SCOTUS has any validity as a fair and impartial high Court to serve the Democracy of the United States!

It must be immediately disbanded and appointed with strictly impartial judges who will serve our democracy with integrity! It really doesn't help SCOTUS's image that at least two of the highly implicated judges in this corrupted transition have been taking HUGE BRIBES from very powerful conservative people! To make it much worse, they have not reported these huge bribes publicly. Also, the Chief Justice has failed to take any 204 disciplinary actions against them and may be one of the perpetrators. He wrote the absurd Absolute Immunity decision for the court! It is now time for Biden, in one of his last acts to save our democracy from becoming a Fascist Autocratic Dictatorship, to disband the Court with his newly granted powers that he received from SCOTUS in the Immunity Decision. If not that, at least appoint four new judges to SCOTUS and have the Senate ratify them before his term ends in January 2025.

SUMMARIES of CASES AGAINST TRUMP

First there was the E. Jean Carroll sexual assault cases resulting in $88.3 million in damages. It is under appeal and may take years to conclude the results.

Then there was the NY Attorney General, Letitia James, suit against the Trump organization for business fraud ending in February 2024 with a judgement of $355 million plus interest total nearly a half of a billion dollars. He was supposed to post that amount in a surety bond during appeal but got off for about $175,000. It is under appeal. Originally it had appeared that the court could have seized Trump tower and other properties if the surety bond not been paid by a certain date. Why that didn't happen seems to be a gross misjudgment of the system. There is no clear explanation for that.

Then followed the case involving 34 felony charges stemming from alleged fraud, election subversion and obstruction when Trump made payments of $130,000 to a porn star to cover up a rape charge just before the 2016 election and shortly after the Oct 7th Access Hollywood tape revelation about Trump bragging about grabbing women's private parts.

A similar story was squelched when the Enquirer magazine used a "catch and kill" method to hide it from public view.
Both are illegal campaign contributions. That judgement   205 was a conviction of all 34 felony counts by a unanimous decision by a jury of his peers in NY state on May 30, 2024. Instead of immediately pronouncing a verdict and sentencing the defendant, this judge set that date for July 11, 2024 - just 4 days before the start of the GOP nominating convention. What nonsense is that? Trump broke every rule of conduct in court and should have been cast into jail at least 6 times for gross violations of his parole terms and conditions. He constantly abraded the judge, his family, his court clerk, his daughter and

cast aspersions upon the jury. Any one of these acts should have landed him in jail until the conclusion of the trial.

The judgement was later delayed until September 18, 2024 - shortly before the elections. Does any of this make any sense regarding our justice system? He should have been sent to jail no later than a week after the end of the trial and the guilty verdict on 34 counts of felony! Trump has ABSOLUTLY NO OBLIGATION TO RUN FOR PRESIDENT, but he has every obligation to abide by rulings and pronouncements of a court. If a court says he must go to jail, HE MUST GO TO JAIL. PERIOD, FULL STOP! Don't you know? Every schoolteacher knows that when a bully acts out in class, he/she must apply disciplinary actions immediately lest the child grow to be some sort of deviant. This person is presumed to be an adult. Apparently, he failed to receive proper discipline as a child so must be dealt with as an adult - TAKEN OUT OF THE PUBLIC REALM FOR THE GOOD OF THE REST OF SOCIETY AND HUMANITY! It is too late just to speak to him about his behavior and hope for the best. He is clearly an unacceptable abrogation of the norms and mores of a functioning society and must be severely curtailed. PERIOD!

PROJECT 2025 and DICTATORSHIP
Now, if you thought that everything that has proceeded this has been strange, you ain't seen "Nutin" yet! Some months 206   ago, I ran into an obscure document called Project 2025 - or the 2025 Presidential Transition Project. It was a 900-page document presumably concocted by some members of the Heritage Society. In fact, under Paul Dan's leadership, over 110 former Trump administration officials were involved in writing project 2025. Even reading just a few pages of it scared the HELL out of me. I literally SH-T in my pants. The terrible consequences that were spelled out made me fear for the future of America as well as the entire world if this lunatic was able to be elected again! HOLY SHIT BATMAN! IS IT THE

JOKER ALL OVER AGAIN? WHERE'S THE BAT SIGNAL? Trump now tries to claim that he has nothing to do with Project 2025 or its projected implementation! HOLY BAT SHIT!

Hang on folks. You thought that you had seen the most bizarre events in your life? "Fasten your seat belts, it's going to be a bumpy ride". There was the Biden - Trump debate on 6/27/24. Everyone thought that Biden would totally spike Trump in this debate. Biden went into preparation nearly a week before. Trump seemed to do no planning whatsoever. To say the least, it seemed to be a total disaster for Biden. Much of the time he just stared at Trump (like a ghost or skeleton) in total disbelief. Trump lied so fluently throughout that he came across as the person that was on top of every situation. The truth is that everything that he said was an out-and-out lie. Even though he managed to stay silent while Biden spoke, most of the time he didn't answer the questions that were presented to him. That normally would have dis-qualified him, but to his base it was pure "Red Meat".

Biden, instead of looking on with a very gaunt face of alarm, should have just smiled knowingly during Trump's lies and then responded with something like "Well, there goes another of his more than 40 thousand lies!" "The man is just incapable of ever telling the truth." "How can you ever trust someone who clearly is a habitual liar!" A pathological liar can never be trusted in any position of power - certainly not in the White 207 House! Biden would have won the day. The results appeared to be so bad for Biden that even his most loyal news people on MSMBC, (like Rachel Maddow and Chris Hayes) were crucifying him immediately after the debate.

That not being bad enough, they, and a chorus of many others like Jennifer Psaki, set up a circular firing squad shooting at Biden for nearly a month afterward. It was one of the most disgusting, detrimentally destructive things that I had ever experienced. America cried out; STOP ALREADY! What in HELL are you thinking? Do you really want Trump to get elected? If not, you are sure not doing anything to stop him. You are shooting Biden in the foot and everywhere else!!

Meanwhile the 34 times convicted felon who planned and implemented a 1/6/21 deadly coup attempt to overthrow our government had the entire MAGA CRIME SYNDICATE cheering him on towards victory! That's why if I have said it once, I have said it a thousand times; "Democrats go to a street fight with soup spoons rather than AR15s and brass knuckles." This, is despite the realization that this election would end our democracies forever, is not a time to be singing Kumbaya, but fighting like HELL to stop this Traitorous Fascist Autocratic Dictator! What in HELL were the news media thinking? Did they have a workable alternative plan? NO! Were they being paid by the MAGA NATIONAL CRIME SYNDICATE headed up by its crime BOSS? Who knows? I've never, ever seen such a stupid reaction just to get ratings and more corporate revenue.

GOP CONVENTION and FIASCO

Finally, that was interrupted by the GOP Convention starting on 7/15/2024 and running until that Friday. During that convention, Trump nominated J. D. Vance to run as his Vice President. Now, JD was a "Never Trump" in 2017. He called Trump "America's Hitler" and a "moral disaster" then. So, 208 what allows people, who obviously knew how bad Trump would be for America at one time, to fall in line with him later in time? Sounds to me like a very serious lack of spine or character! Who needs people like that in American politics? Go figure! We need LEADERS, not FOLLOWERS! Biden was truly a leader and perhaps one of the Nation's most productive and most dedicated. Look at everything that he accomplished for America during the most trying of times. He had to deal with stopping COVID 19 and passed very productive bills in the very trying times that were dominated by MAGA politics!

BIDEN'S BOMBSHELL

Well, one way or another, Biden, after a long weekend with COVID at Rehoboth Beach, Delaware, decided to drop out of the race and backed Kamala Harris as the designated nominee to run for President. That turned out to be very interesting.

Prior to that there seemed to be a large amount of skepticism about her position. There must have been a whale of a lot of pent-up frustration about Biden. Perhaps, the constant MAGA propaganda about his age was very effective. That announcement was like a shot out of a cannon. The Harris campaign took off like a rocket! Seven thousand volunteers suddenly skyrocketed to over 128,000 in a week. Her candidacy raised over $200 million in the first week. She seems to have generated such a response in young voters who had been reluctant to back Biden for many reasons – not the least of which was his support of Netanyahu against Gaza. Being part Black and Asian, she also seemed to fire a spark in those two groups. Of course, being a woman, she sparked a huge response in what amounts to 50% of our population. Oh, there just might be another huge factor. The news media has been spending a large amount of time exposing the 2025 Project. It's damn scary and is beginning to get to normal parts of our population and they are beginning to get very worried! They finally see that there may be very serious 209 consequences to his being able to win back the White House!

Lest I forget. There may very well be another very dramatic factor. It's the selection of J. D. Vance for the MAGA V P. He's been on the campaign trail ever since the GOP convention. America has suddenly discovered that he has, not just un-orthodox, but extremely weird and very warped views about the roles of women and the family. No one should ever get divorced even if in a very abusive marriage. Families without children should have far less rights and influence than those with children. He calls women without children, "cat ladies". This is just the tip of the iceberg. There are so many more quirks that it is impossible to mention them here. His newly discovered quirks have the Trump campaign with very severe "Buyer's Remorse"! What to do, what to do? Buckle your seat belts, it's going to be a very bumpy ride from here on!

SOME CLOSING THOUGHTS

What are we really talking about here? Or, perhaps I should say, WHO are we really talking about here? We are talking about a womanizer, a rapist, a cheat, a thief, a con man, a 34-time convicted felon, a fraud, a tax cheat, a man who has committed business fraud been fined by NY State for nearly half a billion dollars, a failed businessman, a grifter who hawks cheap tennis shoes for $500, a promoter of a dubious Trump University that had to be disbanded. Yes, the list goes on and is too extensive to enumerate here!

Let me ask you, the American public, one simple question. If you were just one of these things, do you think that you would have a shot at being the president of ANY company in the United States? HELL, NO! Even a small, local company would have vetted you enough that you wouldn't even get a return phone call and certainly nowhere near an interview! Is one half of America gullible? Would any of you want to have your

210 18-year-old daughter date this person? Would any of you want this person as your minister in your church or synagogue? Would any of you want this kind of person to be your financial advisor? Would you want this person to be a schoolteacher for your child's class? (Talk about Vance's family values!) In what universe would you even consider such a person to be a trusted friend, advisor or confidant? Does he have any morals that you would be proud to associate with or praise? Would he be one to inspire you to greater acts for Civilization or Humanity? Wouldn't you just love to be known as the person always tagging along with the bully that

constantly makes up childish derogatory names to harass other people he doesn't like? I bet you would NOT! GROW UP CHILD!

The world is far more sophisticated than following a Childish Bully Brat! Who in their right minds would stoop so low that they would follow a little boy that is throwing rocks at everyone else because he is not capable of succeeding on his own merit. Apparently, he feels that he must put everyone else down to try to make himself look more successful. That is classic behavior for a very insecure Bully to try to appear bigger or better than he deserves. Very successful people don't have to be constantly bragging about their real (or perceived) accomplishments. They are known for their significant successes and achievements. Such a person is Joe Biden! GROW UP, WORLD! Many of you took a class in psychology and know these desperate signs so very well!

Now a word to the (so called) men of the former GOP party! GET SOME BALLS ON!! Listen to Hans and Franz and get Pumped up! Surely, after all these years of your self-flagellation and humiliation, when you go home to your families, they look at you like a "Girly Man"! Where is the spine that you all had before this total imposter and con man came along? Where is your pride in the mightiest, and most free democratic nation of all time? Where is your pride in   211 this nation where 100,000's of your fellow citizens gave up their lives to save you and are now resting in graves all over Europe? They gave up their lives to stop the forerunner of your insane "dictator" that you are so clingy to, like "sheep" following herd behavior. Just a word of caution!

Pledging fealty to a foreign adversary or leader of an enemy of the United States used to be considered as an act of TREASON and was punishable by death! If you all are so in love with Putin or Kim Jung-un, then please, be my guest and moves to those lovely dictatorships and spend the rest of your lives in their miserable prisons. See if anyone in America will negotiate to bring you home. It's bloody un-likely!

WHAT is it about RULES and LYING?

So much of the MAGA mantra deals with encouragement to break rules and to either LIE or be totally accepting of LIES! Let's look at a very simple question. While in your car, would you deliberately run a stop sign or a traffic light? Would you do it because you can? Would you do it because you are a free spirit and can do whatever you want? Would you do it because no one is going to tell you what you can or cannot do? Would You do it because some hero of yours told you that you could or should do it? NO? Why not? Because you, hopefully, have enough sense to know that you will likely be killed or will kill someone else! Aha! There can be very dire consequences if you disobey traffic laws or just plain common sense. This is like the phrase that you can't ignore the laws of nature without suffering severe consequences. You can't exceed the prescribed speed going around a curve or your car will likely fly off the road and down a steep ravine or into a stone wall. You have learned that while growing up, from practical experience, or being taught in school. Perhaps a science teacher drummed that into your head.

212   So, why would you avoid getting a COVID 19 vaccine shot to keep you from getting that extremely terrible disease and likely dying from it? Just because some clown told you that the shots were poison or that COVID 19 didn't really exist? Just for spite? Because of this kind of totally sinister propaganda by the MAGA Crime Syndicate, 70% more Republicans died from COVID 19 than Democrats! Because the MAGA-duped crowds believed the diabolical MAGA LIES, at least 500,000 GOP deaths occurred that should have been prevented! Because you believed that the democrats would somehow benefit from you taking those shots, you were going

to spite them and not give them the propaganda win – and DIED for it! Unfortunately, it all goes back to "you cannot cheat the laws of Nature, or you will pay the price" (often, with your own lives!)

LAWS

I know I've talked about this often before, but apparently it isn't controversial enough or outrageous enough for it to stick to your brains. Laws were developed over many years of experience by observing the results of many trials of new behaviors. In essence, they are the beneficial distillation of years of people trying to get along with others as well as with nature and somehow making the two be compatible. Like laws of nature, there are dire consequences if they are ignored or intentionally violated. Congress doesn't just write laws for the fun of it. Neither were the tenets of the Constitution written just for a lark! They are how humans can live closely together and not kill each other or conquer each other as a result. Most importantly of all, they are the BASIS by which humans can TRUST each other to live near each other. When someone or a group, like the MAGA NATIONAL CRIME SYNDICATE intentionally breaks the laws, they are deliberately trying to destroy TRUST and to shred every ability for Society and Humanity to co-exist. They are Terrorists and they are Traitors, plain and simple! They have a goal to destroy not only your lives but those of your families from now and FOREVER!

Guess what. Fascist Dictatorship is the result, and it will   213 have so many laws and edicts that it will make your head spin! So, if you are in the mood to ignore laws, you will be severely disappointed. Those new laws will be strictly enforced without exception. There is no going back after that is done. It's essentially forever! In this case, it is in the form of a 900-page document called "Project 2025". Never ever vote for any of the people who are associated with that document. They are the MAGA NATIONAL CRIME SYNDICATE! They are headed by TRUMP (Putin's Puppet) and Putin (a very dangerous enemy of the free and fair United States). This election is your very last chance to save yourselves and the entire free world! Don't blow it! VOTE BLUE! VOTE HARRIS and WALZ.

LIES

Now for the problem with LIES! When you see an ad on TV that says that product XYX is a magic cure for severe kidney disease, you are curious enough to explore it further. Based upon what you saw, you were convinced by "good authority" that it was effective, so you bought it. What you found out (far too late) was that the "good authority" was a lie, and you then died from its use. That is just one case of how a lie can be very detrimental even to the extent of your death. I could cite hundreds more of such examples but by now you have gotten the message. LIES CAN KILL YOU if you believe them. The perpetrator can say, "You didn't have to buy it or use it"!

Unfortunately, we are very trusting people. Do you see? The truth is only one line between point A and point B. Only one! The truth! There can be thousands of lines between points A and B that are not the truth but may look like or sound like the TRUTH! A very large fraction of these may kill you or place you in a terrible situation that may be entirely untenable. Such a lie would be that Trump has your best interests at heart and that MAGA and he are the real Patriots. It turns out that this 214 LIE will either kill you or totally ruin your life and the lives of your entire family for a very long time. The result of your believing this lie is a Fascist Authoritarian Dictatorship that will rob you of your earnings, your freedoms, and eventually your lives! It is a lie whose results are irreversible and cannot be adjudicated to your benefit in any court. Talk to Brittney Griner or Navalny (who was killed in a Siberian prison).

Essentially, everything that you have ever known will be gone or removed from you. All freedoms, joy, happiness, work, knowledge, fun, family reunions, vacations, abundant friends will all just suddenly disappear never to return, and you cannot do a DAMN THING ABOUT IT - BECAUSE OF THE GESTOPO, (like private militias that will constantly monitor your every word, follow your every movement, and decide if you are allowed to work ever again or not). They are likely to separate members of your family, and some may be deported or placed in terrible concentration camps. Crying won't help. Bribery? Perhaps a little, until you are cashed out with no possible work available to you. Again, NEVER, EVER vote for anyone associated with THE MAGA NATIONAL CRIME SYNDICATE! It is totally unimaginable why anyone would (not just willingly, but eagerly) strive to live under a dictatorship rather than any other form of government! Just look at Russia. Be very honest now. Would any of you want to live in Russia? America's government by the people may be slow, or inefficient, but it isn't the HELL of a Russia or a FASCIST Authoritarian Dictatorship! Get real, folks. GET VERY, VERY REAL - ASAP!

EPILOGUE

LIAR, LIAR, LIAR, LIAR, LIAR, LIAR, LIAR, LIAR, LIAR

The man lied 30,000 times during the four years in office. He has lied at least 65,000 times since he started campaigning in 2015! It used to be that a single lie from a candidate would

blow them out of any race immediately after it was brought 215 to light. God help you if you are caught lying when applying for a job! Most relationships end with just one LIE! I guess that 65,000 lies might be considered to be normal now! If you can't remember anything else, REMEMBER THIS! Lies destroy trust faster than anything else on earth! How can 340 million people be able to trust even one word of this despicable person after just one lie – much less after 65,000 lies? For GOD's sake it's been 10 years that we have been hearing them. Like my girlfriend, I've heard the same old stories so many times that I can tell them by heart since they have gotten so old and worn out. Stories aren't lies, so they don't destroy trust, but if they were lies they should get very old after just the 2nd or 3rd time. Most people would be done with the teller after they've heard them just a few times.

This man is completely devoid of any reason for living in a well- balanced humane society. If you were to rate him on his reason for being or for his contributions to the enhancement or our world on a scale was 0 to 10, he would rate worse than -30! This is because he is actually more destructive to any society than he ever pretended to be helpful. He brags about building great THINGS, but he is in reality a TAKER! There are references in the Bible of the 7 deadly sins and the kinds of people who are totally involved in all of them. Those chapters describe this person in every detail: Lust, Wrath, Gluttony, Avarice, Greed, Slothfulness, Envy, Pride and Deceitful. These can be distilled down to 7 statements that describe him to a Tee. 1 A proud look. 2. A lying tongue. 3. Hands that shed innocent blood. 4. A heart that devises wicked plans. 5. Feet that are swift in running to evil. 6. A false witness who speaks lies. 7. One who sows discord among brethren. (Proverbs 6:16-19). Look at that last list very hard! Listen to the things he says at his campaign rally's. Are they not exactly what you are hearing every day?

216   Let me remind you of just one very serious example of item 7. on that list that he and his VP candidate have been propagating every day since September 10, 2024 – two weeks ago. They are stating that the 15,000 legal Haitian immigrants that have moved to Springfield, OH are stealing their neighbor's cats and dogs and are eating them. This totally fabricated lie has been debunked by the town's mayor, chief of police, newspapers, and the GOP Governor of the state – over

and over again! The immediate result of these hateful lies is that the lives of these Haitian people have been put into mortal danger. There have been many bomb threats that have closed schools and public buildings in the city. Most of the Haitians are now afraid to leave their homes because of possible violence that might befall them. A normal person, would realize the danger that they are causing for innocent people and immediately stop the lying. These two immoral people, instead have doubled down and are telling even more lies to make the situation far worse! Is that the kind of person any one of you would want to be in control of your safety and well-being? Safety is the Presidents # 1 Job!

Let me finish by stating a list of beneficial characteristics that he simply doesn't have. He has no cat or dog, conscience or empathy. He has no love of music, literature, books, plays, or drama. He has no love of duty or responsibility. He has no respect for law and order, police or military. He has no respect for veterans either alive or dead. He has no respect for honor, bravery, service, duty, endeavor, work, progress or sacrifice. He has no respect for humanity, individualism, freedom or choices. He has no respect for strife, perseverance or survivorship. He has no respect for anyone but himself – not even his wife or children. He has no respect for anyone else except Putin, Kim Jong-un, Xi Jinping of China – all dictators. That tells you a lot!

His goals are avarice, greed, hate, division and destruction. 217 He glorifies destruction as something to brag about ignoring the fact that destruction is the easiest thing in the universe to do. Entropy does all of the hard part of destruction. All you have to do is "pull the trigger". Building something of value is the only thing you can brag about! It requires planning, negotiating, financing, employing, dedication and hard work! This man seems to believe in perpetual motion machines because he seems to expect the world to owe him a constant and overly abundant living with all of the king's riches thrown in for good measure! What a profoundly, totally worthless vessel that has been cast upon our fate and the possibly terrible fate for America. We must all pray fervently for the survival of our very civilization as well as for our now abundant freedoms and good pleasures. GOD BLESS AMERICA! GOD BLESS OUR VOTES!

The next two pages are left blank for notes.